The **HEALING** Bond

Treating Addictions in Groups

BOOKS BY
RONALD L. ROGERS AND CHANDLER SCOTT McMILLIN

Don't Help: A Guide to Working With the Alcoholic
The Twelve Steps Revisited: AA and the Disease of Alcoholism
(with Morris A. Hill)
Freeing Someone You Love From Alcohol and Other Drugs

A NORTON PROFESSIONAL BOOK

The **HEALING** Bond

Treating Addictions in Groups

Ronald L. Rogers

CLINICAL DIRECTOR,
BALTIMORE RECOVERY CENTER

Chandler Scott McMillin

DIRECTOR, ADDICTION TREATMENT CENTER
SUBURBAN HOSPITAL, BETHESDA

W·W· NORTON & COMPANY
New York   *London*

First Edition

Library of Congress Cataloging-in-Publication Data

Rogers, Ronald.
  The healing bond : treating addictions in groups / Ronald L.
Rogers and C. Scott McMillin. – 1st ed.
    p. cm.
  "A Norton professional book."
    1. Substance abuse – Relapse – Prevention. 2. Goal (Psychology)
3. Self-help groups. I. McMillin, C. Scott. II. Title.
RC564.R64   1989   89-34185
616.86′05 – dc20   CIP

ISBN-0-393-70083-6 [HBK.]
ISBN-0-393-70088-7 [PBK.]

W. W. Norton & Company, Inc., 500 Fifth Avenue, New York, N.Y. 10110
W. W. Norton & Company Ltd., 37 Great Russell Street, London WC1B 3NU

1 2 3 4 5 6 7 8 9 0

For our families, with love

CONTENTS

AUTHORS' NOTE

In writing a book in which most of
the information applies equally to
people of both sexes, we were faced
with the dilemma of sex-specific pro-
nouns. While we don't like referring
to the alcoholic as "he" or "him"
throughout the book, our language
at present leaves only the awkward
"he/she" choice. We have used the ge-
neric "he" instead of "he/she." No offense intended; it's simply for reada-
bility.

ACKNOWLEDGMENTS

AS ALWAYS, THERE ARE hundreds of people who have made contributions to the ideas and techniques described in this book, and we must apologize for not naming them individually. There are two, however, whom we must credit explicitly: Robert Markel for his guidance and representation, and Susan Barrows for her invaluable editorial skills and vision.

Like everyone who works with groups, our approach has been influenced by the work of pioneers such as Irving Yalom and Wilfred Bion. And the chronic disease model which forms the basis of our approach to addictions is a direct result of our reading of the work of Dr. James Milam, particularly *Under the Influence*. To those of us working with alcoholics, this book is invaluable.

The HEALING Bond

Treating Addictions in Groups

CHAPTER 1

A BRIEF HISTORY OF ADDICTIONS GROUPS

WHEN THE TREATMENT of alcoholism as a disease was in its infancy – only a few decades ago – clinicians based their approaches to group therapy on training they had received in other fields.

A significant percentage of these clinicians had backgrounds in traditional mental health. Accordingly, their methods were derived from psychotherapy, and their treatment programs bore marks of the classic psychiatric milieu.

In such programs, group therapy sessions were routinely directed by mental health practitioners, and were oriented towards helping members gain insight into the supposed psychodynamic roots of their problems with alcohol. Considerable emphasis was placed on learning to express feelings within the group setting.

Sessions were often unstructured, to permit the group to meet the needs of individual members. Participants were advised to bring their emotional problems to the group, which would offer help in coping with them. Most of these difficulties involved relationships with other people. Group members were taught to examine their own behavior, as well as that of others, in psychodynamic terms. The group presumably aided this process of self-examination by providing warmth, support, and feedback.

Other clinicians, less traditional but still psychologically minded, favored transpersonal or client-centered approaches. Gestalt therapy, transactional analysis, and family therapy became fixtures in some programs. Despite their dissimilarities, all retained an emphasis on expressing feelings and on understanding behavior in psychodynamic terms. In the family-centered approach, the focus shifted from the alcoholic as the "designated patient" to the complex relations among family members. Alcoholism was thus viewed as the product of a dysfunctional family system rather than an inadequate personality.

Though each model characterized the alcoholic or addict as suffering from a "disease," that term was used only in its loosest sense. The dynamics of addiction were still viewed as primarily intrapsychic (in analytic models) or interpersonal (in family models). The *physiology* of addiction received only superficial acknowledgment. The alcoholic might be told that alcohol was bad for his liver, but therapy groups were dominated by discussions of psychodynamics.

Another source of clinical staff was the parallel field of narcotics addiction. These clinicians were firmly rooted in the theory and practice of *confrontation*. To them, addiction was the natural result of a dependent personality relying on drugs to cope with unpleasant feelings. This underlying character weakness was inevitably armored with rigid defenses. The success of treatment depended on the group's ability to strip away these layers of defense until the addict stood revealed. Once able to express genuine "gut-level" emotion, and to relate to others in a nonmanipulative fashion, the addict would presumably no longer require drugs to cope with reality. The emotional nature of this approach meant that intellectual understanding – so important to the psychoanalyst – had to be disparaged as "head-tripping."

"Hot seat" groups appeared, in which one member found himself "It" while the others gave him highly confrontive "feedback" – usually regarding his unwillingness to "open up" or be honest with the group – and struggled with his defenses. Once again, the idea that alcoholism was a disease was of secondary importance. The group's primary concern was with the alcoholic's *character*.

Perhaps the largest segment of the new clinicians came from

a source unfamiliar to medicine: Twelve Step fellowships such as Alcoholics and Narcotics Anonymous. Through their experience of recovery, former patients themselves grew interested in professional counseling. Quite naturally, sessions run by recovering alcoholics resembled AA meetings. A premium was placed on self-disclosure – the counselor, revealing his or her personal experience, would spur similar revelations from the members. The session itself might even be organized around one of the AA's Twelve Steps. Therapy, like an AA meeting, was seen as a forum where alcoholics could share "experience, strength, and hope" with one another. The spiritual tone which accompanied many AA meetings carried over to therapy groups.

Eventually, the various models began to merge. Treatment programs adopted features of each. A single program might require patients to attend AA-style discussion groups, hot seat confrontations, gestalt workshops, and psychodynamic therapy sessions. Family programs were similarly diverse.

Our travels through the world of addictions treatment have led us to speculate that practically every form of group yet devised is being used to treat alcoholism at some facility in America. We have found gestalt groups, values clarification groups, recreation and relaxation groups, music and art groups, sex-role discussion groups, couples and conjoint and single family and multiple family groups, vocational and avocational and spiritual and nonbeliever's groups, stress reduction and biofeedback and guided imagery groups. We even discovered a program which emphasizes a group entitled "Uncle Petey's Storybook Hour," where a therapist reads aloud to an audience of addicts seated at his feet like schoolchildren.

All of this, of course, is done in the name of treating the disease of alcoholism and drug dependency. And therein, we believe, lies something of a contradiction.

We simply do not see how anyone could expect a chronic disease to respond to some of these approaches.

In the first place, alcoholism and drug dependency are physiological in origin. They are probably hereditary. They do not, we believe, trace their existence to flaws in the alcoholic's character. Instead, they produce changes in the way the addict thinks, feels, and acts.[1] We have seen little persuasive evidence linking alcoholism to a particular personality profile which exists prior to the onset of drinking. In fact, good prospective research seems to *contradict* such assumptions.[2] Realizing this, we have come to the conclusion that even if we were to develop a method for transforming the alcoholic's personality to its polar opposite, he or she would probably still be alcoholic.

We also find no convincing evidence that alcoholism is brought about by dysfunctional family systems. Families can encourage or discourage drinking and drug use; they can indulge in enabling or provoking behavior; they can respond effectively or ineffectively to alcohol or drug related problems. But even in this respect it seems to us that the family is emphatically the *victim* of the disease, instead of its creator.

We believe that the treatment of addictions requires a new approach to group therapy, based on an understanding of the disease process. We think that in many ways the philosophy, values, and techniques of psychotherapy are inadequate for this purpose. In other words, little progress has been made in fitting treatment to the disease *as we now understand it*.

Our understanding of addiction has changed immensely over the past few decades. Our methods of treatment have not always kept pace. As a result, alcoholics and addicts attend sophisticated lectures in which they learn that they suffer from a chronic, progressive and physiological disease, followed by group therapy in which they are treated as though they have a personality disorder. If alcoholism is indeed a disease, then our obligation is to treat it as such. Otherwise, we simply perpetuate the myths and stereotypes of earlier generations. We *stigmatize* the alcoholic, even as we promise to set him free.

The history of medicine is rife with examples where disease was misidentified as personality disorder. Tuberculosis victims, for instance, were once believed to be exceptionally sensi-

1. See Suggested Reading, especially *Under the Influence* by James Milam.
2. See George Vaillant's *The Natural History of Alcoholism*.

tive and artistic, and young romantics sometimes affected a "consumptive" pallor as proof of their delicate temperament. Of course, we now know that TB has little to do with emotional sensitivity. Perhaps fifty years ago, when we knew so little about addictive illness and its causes, our flaws could be easily excused. But our fund of information has increased exponentially in the past few decades. To persist in attributing alcoholism solely to environmental or psychodynamic factors, in light of recent research, would be absurd. As a result of such changes, treatment methods have altered dramatically—except, we think, in the realm of group therapy. There, the alcoholic too often remains "psychologically inadequate," his disease misidentified as a character disorder.

Group therapy has not always been seen as the exclusive province of psychiatry. Groups have been used with considerable success in the treatment of such chronic diseases as diabetes, cancer and tuberculosis. Each, like alcoholism, was without available cure. Treatment aimed at *arresting* the disease process. For instance, in the case of diabetes, treatment might involve insulin supplements. For heart patients, medication regimens might accompany reduced workload and restricted diet.

For the alcoholic, treatment is simpler than most: Avoid alcohol and similar drugs. Adjust to the resulting changes in lifestyle.

Alcoholics, of course, vary enormously in personality, background and ability. Nevertheless, they also have much in common: principally, the experience of alcoholism, and the need to recover from it. For example, every victim of alcoholism or drug addiction has to make several basic changes in behavior and attitude, no matter how otherwise advantaged or disadvantaged he or she may be. AA and NA are built around this commonality. Rather than dwelling on differences between oneself and others, the AA member learns to focus on the universal themes of recovery. These themes can be heard at any AA meeting: "We all suffered from alcoholism. We all did things of which we are ashamed. We all had to start over. We all had setbacks. We all needed outside help." And perhaps most importantly: "We all had to do things we didn't want to do, in order to recover."

We believe the group—rather than the individual—is the best instrument for producing and supporting change. However, in order to use groups effectively, we must see them as considerably greater than the sum of their parts. Because recovery requires considerable changes in behavior, we must study how groups accomplish tasks. We must develop within the group setting an atmosphere conducive to measurable, specific personal change. And most importantly, once we've done so, we need to get out of the way, so that the group can treat its own members.

If our approach differs from traditional models, it is perhaps most apparent in one respect: We don't seek to treat addictions in groups. *We strive instead to create groups strong enough to treat addictions without us.*

The group, we believe, is better than the individual clinician when it comes to assisting its own members as they complete the tasks of recovery. In fact, for this purpose, we think a solid working group can be of more value than the best therapist in the world.

In the remaining text, we will outline a method for developing the "working group" and offer practical exercises in identifying group process. We also look briefly at Alcoholics Anonymous itself as a working group: a classic example of the breed, to be admired and even emulated by professionals. However, before turning to the practicalities of treating addictions in groups, let us briefly review the chronic disease model. (For further background, we encourage you to make use of the Suggested Reading List at the conclusion of the text.)

The essential assumption of *the chronic disease* model is that alcoholism and drug dependency should be grouped with diseases that are chronic, progressive, primary, and potentially fatal.

Chronic means long-lasting. *Progressive* implies an accumulation of signs and symptoms and increasing morbidity. A *primary* disease has its own etiology, course, and prognosis, and does not owe its existence to the presence of another disorder. As for *fatality*, if we add together the medical and nonmedical consequences of alcoholism and drug dependency, we might find that addiction is our nation's number one killer.

Addictive disease can be divided into first-, second-, and third-order symptoms. First-order symptoms are the hallmarks of physiological adaptation. They include adaptive tolerance (diminished response to doses of a drug) and dependence (the presence of withdrawal symptoms in response to decreasing levels of the drug). They may also include the various forms of pathological organ change that accompany chronic ingestion of alcohol, narcotics, cocaine, etc.

Second-order symptoms are ways of thinking and behaving that are a reaction to the disease (or, more properly, to the first order symptoms) — for example, the various defense mechanisms that surround drinking or drug use. Denial, rationalization, externalization, and minimizing are the four most common.

Third-order symptoms include negative feelings that result from the experience of the disease (depression, mood swings) and from the patient's perception of the illness. Because alcoholism and drug dependency are stigmatized, third-order symptoms include a degree of shame and remorse that heart patients don't normally experience. Because patients perceive alcoholism and drug addiction as accusation rather than diagnosis, they constantly reinterpret their symptoms, offering alternative explanations which lead to conflict with and isolation from others. For example, many alcoholics mistakenly blame their wives and children for their drinking. When family members react with guilt, hurt, or defensiveness, it gives birth to a cycle of chronic antagonism and discontent.

All three levels are normally addressed during the treatment process. First-order symptoms such as withdrawal and organ deterioration are dealt with during detoxification and medical care. Second- and third-order symptoms are explained in the

context of the disease process, rather than as the result of psychosocial maladjustment or character inadequacy.
Treatment has four primary goals:

1. *Educating the patient:* As with any disease which we can arrest but not cure, there is a strong emphasis on teaching the patient about the illness. This is important because the patient is ultimately responsible for following through with the treatment regimen, and will therefore determine its success or failure.
2. *Self-diagnosis:* This is the point where the alcoholic or addict, after examining his or her experience, concludes that he or she indeed suffers from the disease. Self-diagnosis is the source of lasting motivation for recovery. Most addicts enter treatment because of an external crisis in a key area of life — career, health, family, legal, etc. This crisis opens a "window" in their denial system. If no further attitudinal change occurs, that window will close as the crisis fades — and the patient's motivation for sobriety will fade with it. Thus, the key to continued recovery lies in acceptance of an underlying disease process which requires ongoing attention to insure against future crises.
3. *Involvement in effective treatment:* The alcoholic or addict is introduced to the various methods of treatment — from Twelve Step fellowships like Alcoholics or Narcotics Anonymous to relaxation techniques and relapse prevention groups. From these, patient and clinician develop and implement a "prescription" for recovery — a treatment regimen designed to maximize chances for sobriety and minimize the potential for relapse.
4. *Assumption of personal responsibility* for ongoing treatment. The alcoholic or addict comes to understand that success depends largely on his or her willingness to continue in the treatment process. Abstinence from alcohol and drugs must become an unconditional behavior — something which the addict maintains in the face of changing circumstances and fluctuating moods. As long as he or she operates on the assumption that certain conditions excuse or justify a return

to chemicals, then relapse will continue to occur, and the addict will remain vulnerable to the disease. Thus, the help that's available – from AA to counseling – is effective only to the extent that the patient assumes responsibility for making use of it.

Now, let's begin our discussion of groups that work and groups that don't. We'll start by establishing a working vocabulary of group process.

CHAPTER 2

THE VOCABULARY OF GROUPS

PEOPLE WHO VALUE clarity often recoil at the language of humanistic psychology.

"It's a linguistic catastrophe," one semanticist complained to us. "People mix the abstract with the concrete. Authors toss around terms like 'self-esteem' and 'self-actualization,' which invariably mean ten different things to ten different people. In that respect, psychology is as bad as philosophy and theology."

Since we don't want to perpetuate such difficulties, we have decided to devote this chapter to defining our terminology. We make no claim that our definitions are absolute; we simply want you to know what we are talking about when we refer to a particular term.

Here, then, is our vocabulary of group process.

GOALS OF TREATMENT

Obviously, treatment for any illness is designed to achieve certain goals, which should improve the patients condition.

For example, goals for a diabetic might involve regulation of blood sugar through insulin supplements and diet. For an emphysemic, regular breathing treatments along with abstinence from cigarettes would be essential.

In addictions treatment, there is one overriding goal: impressing upon the patient the importance of permanent abstinence from alcohol and other drugs. This larger goal, however, is usually broken down into more manageable components, which are:

1. Educating the patient about the causes, dynamics, and characteristics of the disease;
2. Helping the patient to *self-diagnose* (identify the disease in his or her experience);
3. Teaching the patient effective methods for self-treatment of the disease;
4. Convincing him or her of the importance of taking personal responsibility for ongoing abstinence.

When we concentrate on these goals, the larger objective is achieved.

In comparison, unstructured psychotherapy groups tend to feature multiple goals, which vary from member to member. This puts members in the position of expecting different results from the same group experience.

HOMOGENEOUS VS. HETEROGENEOUS GROUPS

In a homogeneous group, members are included because they have something in common. This in turn becomes the basis for interaction. Alcoholics Anonymous is a classic homogeneous group.

Addictions treatment groups should be homogeneous by *diagnosis*. Traditional psychotherapy groups, by contrast, are often heterogeneous: alcoholics are treated along with schizophrenics, depressives, etc. The only point of commonality is that the members happen to be on the same psychiatric unit.

TASK

A task is a topic of discussion that focuses the group effort on advancing its goals. A task-oriented group is one which exists in order to accomplish a particular goal, such as building a better mousetrap, formulating a policy, or recovering from a disease.

BONDING

Groups begin as collections of individuals. When the group responds as a whole to some stimulus (such as the designated leader), we say it has *bonded*. Bonding may be either positive or negative.

Suppose a group of recovering alcoholics gets together with the idea of supporting each other in abstaining from alcohol. If AA is an indicator, their chances for success are good. The members should experience improvement in their physical and psychological functioning.

But suppose instead that the group bonds around the idea of learning to drink in a controlled fashion. If past experience holds true, we should expect some rather spectacular failures. In terms of the members' overall welfare, the second bonding is emphatically negative.

Members bring their own agendas to group therapy. Once the group bonds, however, an additional factor emerges which contributes powerfully to group behavior: *group process*. The group begins to influence each of its members – for better or for worse.

MENTALITY

As group process develops, groups begin to behave in ways which do not always reflect the conscious intent of the members. We call this the group's *mentality*. This mentality is often quite obvious to observers, while remaining hidden to the participants.

Suppose you are invited to attend a group where several members praise the group for its value in reconstructing their lives. Their positive attitude is impressive, and you conclude the group is strong and healthy.

After a few sessions, however, you notice that several of the less vocal members appear to be under the influence of alcohol. Rather than addressing these "failures," however, the vocal members continue their discussion, thereby preserving the group's image.

Your impression now changes. You conclude that the group is of little benefit to a significant percentage of the participants. The vocal members are in fact cheerleaders for a losing team.

The mentality of such a group might be expressed as: "Maybe if we *pretend* everything is OK, something will happen to make it true."

CLIMATE

Climate describes the *morale* of the group. There exists both a background and a foreground climate. *Background* climate refers to the attitudes and beliefs members bring to the group. *Foreground* climate reflects their reaction to what happens in the group itself. Background and foreground influence one another. Thus the members influence their group, and the group influences its members.

VALUES

Groups make decisions about the relative importance of many behaviors. These decisions, whether overt or covert, form the group's values.

A group will decide, for example, whether:

1. Total time invested in sessions is more valuable than the quality of the discussion;
2. Being able to depend on a designated leader is more desirable than achieving autonomous functioning;
3. Accomplishing specific goals is more valuable than getting to know other members;
4. Roles assumed by members are fixed, or may change to fit a particular task.

As the group develops these values, they in turn influence interaction and group process. Various *modes* emerge which are associated with these values.

MODE

When a group is engaged in definite activity — be it fighting
with the leader or one another, working on a problem, discussing the weather, sitting silently, or whatever — we say the
group is in a given *mode*.

There are four basic modes found in addictions groups: *helpless, hostile, hopeful expectation*, and *work*. We will discuss
these in the next chapter.

STATUS

Who has authority within the group? Does it flow exclusively from the designated leader? Can authority shift to a certain
member for a specific purpose?

Newly formed groups tend to bestow status based on external standards, and the leader will be the only authority figure.
This changes, however. If the group members get angry with
the leader, they will bestow status on his most vocal critics.
When the group is working, status passes among members,
depending upon their ability to perform the task.

TRADITIONS

Traditions are developed by groups to unify the membership
and to simplify certain processes so that members don't have to
reinvent the wheel. This facilitates decision-making by providing a groundwork of acceptable solutions.

STRUCTURE

Structure is defined by the who, what, when and where of
the group. Structure should facilitate the group's work. If each
member must provide a five-minute report on some issue, then
the group must be long enough to allow this to occur. Certain
structures promote work; others interfere with it.

CULTURE

Once a group bonds, conflict will arise between the dominant mode of the group and the desires of any member who opposes that mode. This is similar to what happens in the formation of a society. The *culture* of a group reflects this conflict.

If the group bonds around abstinence from alcohol, a member who persists in drinking will become an outcast. If a group bonds around the idea that every member should be able to control his or her drinking (as did our society), then an alcoholic—who cannot always achieve this—will be the outcast.

Groups, like larger societies, permit a certain degree of atypical behavior, but there is always conflict between the atypical member and the larger group. This conflict can work for or against treatment of addiction. AA obviously influences alcoholics towards sobriety, through positive peer pressure. The environment of a cocktail lounge, however, encourages alcoholics to resume drinking.

WORK

This is the most important definition, because this is what should happen in a treatment group. *Work is a mode of activity which advances the goals of treatment*, thus bringing the members closer to stable recovery.

We plan to describe the features of "working" and "nonworking" groups in some detail. Let's start by examining what happens in groups that *don't* work.

CHAPTER 3

GROUPS THAT DON'T WORK

AS WE DESCRIBE nonworking groups, it's only fair that we reveal an assumption which underlies much of our approach. We believe that simple willingness to invest time and money in therapy represents little guarantee that a person will actually *use* that therapy to change life for the better. In fact, we've found that much time is in fact devoted to *resisting* change—even if the desire for change is what brought that individual to therapy in the first place.

Groups are no exception. Just as individuals fight making necessary changes in their lives, so, too, do groups bond around various forms of resistance.

Why?

Well, for one thing, change is *difficult*. You have to work at it. There will be setbacks, wrong turns, frustrating delays. Life during such periods may be uncomfortable, even threatening.

So what if change is absolutely necessary? It's still scary. Especially if you find yourself in the position of having to give up something upon which you've grown to depend.

For these and other reasons, any group leader should be prepared to find that much of the energy and creativity of his group is devoted to *avoiding* its supposed therapeutic objectives. Therefore, we believe that 90% of effective group leadership is simply a matter of getting the group to overcome its own natural resistance to work.

When a group is permitted to resist change on a consistent

basis, a secondary phenomenon occurs: Members who *are* motivated for change will begin to drop out. Group leaders, however, routinely misinterpret this. To many leaders, all dropouts are "unmotivated." It seldom enters a leader's mind that the dropout might in fact *want* to change and experiences the group as *interfering* with this goal.

Let's leave the realm of addictions for a moment and listen to the story of a former group therapist who attended an outpatient therapy group, only to become what he himself had always despised – a dropout – after 12 sessions. We'll follow him as he discovers that the group has no intention of meeting his needs, and in fact will *exclude* him.

ALBERT'S STORY

"I went to group therapy for the same reason as most: My own therapist recommended it. I'd been in individual counseling for about five months, trying to decide whether to leave a rotten marriage.

"Like a lot of divorcing people, I was short on bucks. My therapist told me I could join his group for $40. a week, saving myself about $35., and I jumped at the chance. To tell the truth, I wanted to quit therapy altogether, but he felt I wasn't ready.

"So I joined his group. I ought to tell you I was a group leader myself for several years, so I'm familiar with how it works. But I learned something as a member I never learned as a leader: There are groups that do what a textbook would call good therapy but are really wasting time; and group therapy can really be an *obstacle* to change.

"Like most such groups, ours didn't have a stated goal. I suppose the closest anyone ever came to stating a specific purpose was when the leader once commented that we were there to increase our understanding of ourselves. But individual members of the group also had their own agendas. One woman said she was there to learn to communicate better with men – she'd had a couple of husbands, I guess. Another wanted help with her marriage. The guy who made the biggest impression on me was there supposedly to develop the confidence to apply for a new job – he hated his present one. I remember thinking: If he wants a new job, why not go get one? He's got a lot of education. How is sitting in group therapy going to get him a new job? But that's beside the point.

"Anyway, after about three sessions I figured out that our group wasn't one group, but *two*. The three members I just mentioned did 90% of the talking, and I called them the 'Actives.' Even when other members talked, it was usually in response to their prodding. The other six or seven members of the group, myself included, you'd have to call the 'Passives.' We looked pretty bored.

"Here's a typical session. The facilitators – a man and a woman – wouldn't say much at the start. They'd just sit and wait. Pretty soon, the level of anxiety would build in the group, and one of the Actives would say, 'Well, I guess somebody better start this off . . . ' Then the Actives would spend five or ten minutes each bringing us up to date on what had happened in their lives since the last meeting, or maybe confront each other about something the other person had said at the last session, that apparently the Active had been chewing on all week. I found this painfully dull, the very definition of boring.

"Then maybe halfway through the group, the leaders would seem to decide that something had been brought up which was worth their attention. One would jump in with some kind of confrontation, along the lines of 'I don't think you're really telling us how you felt when she said that,' or whatever. The other leader would stay supportive of the person who was getting confronted, so he wouldn't get upset or feel picked on, I suppose. It was like the 'good cop and bad cop' routines on television.

"The second half of the group was always a dialogue between one of the leaders and one of the active members. The Actives took turns being 'it' – they even joked about it – but a Passive never got the limelight.

"Occasionally one of the Actives would confront the Passives with being too quiet, or with being unwilling to share themselves. Sharing was a constant topic in this group. If you weren't sharing, it was because you were 'withholding' or 'out of touch with your feelings.' They were very critical of silence. But outside of brief interchanges, the three Actives did *all* the talking for the group, while the Passives sat and waited.

"Once I was confronted with my lack of participation. It *was* strange, I admit, since I was a trained therapist myself. But when I told the group why I was inactive – essentially because I didn't relate to the problems or 'issues' that the group constantly discussed – they really went after me.

"For example, take the guy who wanted the new job. I pointed out to him as nicely as I could that if he devoted half as much time to looking for a job as he did to talking about it in group therapy, he'd probably be employed elsewhere by now. He said that was a very hostile comment.

"Maybe it was. It was also true.

"The group never seemed to look at the relative accuracy or inaccuracy of any observation. If it seemed critical of the way they behaved, they turned on whoever made the observation. The leaders, who didn't openly criticize me, were nonetheless supportive of the Actives, and seemed to be firmly in that camp.

"As I look back, I can see that what was supposed to be an 'open' group – where anything could be discussed – was in fact *closed* to much of the input of its own members. I now believe that most of the Actives were in the group specifically to *avoid* changing anything.

"In other words, I don't think the lady with the bad marriage wanted out of it, and I doubt that the one who couldn't communicate with men would ever learn how. I know for *damn* sure that one fellow is *still* looking for a new job.

"My dominant reaction in group was: Oh, God, don't let me end up like that . . . sitting in therapy for months or years, doing nothing, getting nowhere.

"I felt they were a bunch of wimps. Yet they were able to completely dominate that group. I guess they couldn't permit anyone to get anywhere, lest it show up their own inadequacies.

"But I was also aware – and this helped fool me for a while – that what the textbook said was *supposed* to happen in group

therapy did in fact happen. People brought up 'issues' which
were important to them. They got feedback. They explored
their feelings and attitudes. They related their present behavior to their upbringing. They interacted with each other, and
I'm sure they improved their morale. They made progress from
time to time. I'm sure some of the members would have called
the group 'helpful.'

"And yet, I am firmly convinced that group was absolutely
dead in the water—and had been, I imagine, for at least a year.

"Of course, the Passives never expressed an opinion. And the
Actives saw the group as productive because they got all the
attention they wanted. The leaders were grossing about $600 a
night, so that probably sweetened the experience for them.

"But to me, this group was all form and no content. So I
decided, for my own benefit, to quit.

"Did you ever try to *quit* a group like that? I heard the same
arguments the therapist had used to get me into the group in
the first place—now delivered with great force and intensity by
both the Actives and the leaders. I was copping out, giving up
on myself, admitting defeat, afraid to open up, avoiding my
feelings.

"What a bunch of nonsense. But at the time, you always
wonder: Are they *right*? Am I blind to my own garbage? Will
this mean I'll be unhappy forever?

"Finally, I was saved by poverty. Nobody could think of a
way for me to pay for the sessions. If I could have signed away
my soul, I'm sure they'd have advised me to do so.

"Looking back, I feel the whole thing was a rip-off. You come
in looking for a solution to some legitimate problem. But the
therapists seduce you into believing that they have some secret
you don't, implying that your life won't work unless you have
their help. The price of that 'secret knowledge' is long-term
therapy. Then, when you've committed yourself, they frustrate
you at every turn. Pretty soon, you've forgotten why you went
into therapy in the first place, because now you work on what
they think is wrong with you. And the amazing thing is that no
matter how experienced you are—no matter how much you
know about groups—you can still get hooked by a bad group.

"It seems to me that if the Actives had really wanted to achieve the goals they said they did, they would have shown more tangible results from all that talking. And if they really *didn't* care about those goals—if they had a secondary agenda, such as remaining safely in the warm, fuzzy group blanket— then everything they talked about in the sessions was just an elaborate defense against change.

"Either way, the group was a joke.

"I believe that anyone who truly intended to change for the better would be forced to drop out in self-defense."

☐   ☐   ☐

We think that Albert's experience typifies that of persons who enter group therapy to find support for positive change, only to discover their group seems to *oppose* such change.

Take a close look at the process of this group as portrayed in Albert's commentary. In the first place, he notes that his group neither bonded around any common task nor set itself a goal towards which to work. In this respect, it was typical of modern "free-form" psychotherapy groups. Often the philosophy behind such taskless groups is that any formal setting of goals would inhibit the ability of the group to respond to its members' needs. Task-oriented discussion, the argument goes, destroys the "spontaneity" of group process and encourages members to suppress certain feelings or facets of personality in order to achieve the designated goal.

All this is true. But it seems to us that change itself is necessarily "task-oriented." Therefore, someone who wants to change his behavior (and thus his lifestyle) would benefit little from a group that does not set and achieve goals. As Albert pointed out, *no one* in his group achieved stated goals. The woman with marital problems discussed the same problems, week after week. The man who wanted a new job seemed to grow less and less able to pursue and obtain one.

Was this because these individuals had not fully committed themselves to change? Yes, in part. But Albert *had* committed himself. The group's reaction to his goal-oriented behavior makes it clear that *the group itself was dedicated to resisting behavioral and attitudinal change by its members.*

Albert also observes that his group had at some point split into two separate factions: one characterized by talk without positive action, the other by silence and passivity. He makes it plain that the activity, in terms of group participation, did not really correlate with measurable progress. Albert himself, a highly motivated group member looking to change his lifestyle, fell in with the "passive" contingent. His passivity resulted not from shyness or unfamiliarity with group therapy but from avoidance of the conflict which he sensed would emerge when he disagreed with the group's accepted beliefs and rationale.

Free-form psychotherapy groups are full of such "Actives." They may be the senior members of such groups, since more change-oriented members have long ago left the fold. They may have established an alliance with the group's designated leaders. The tone of their discussion may give the impression that they are working on important issues. The leaders may continue to "help" the Actives as they struggle. Yet neither Actives nor therapists can demonstrate that the group is accomplishing anything that would justify the time and energy they devote to it.

When Albert nervily confronted the Actives and the leaders with the fact that he couldn't relate to the problems they discussed, he burst a particularly precious bubble: the illusion that the group was of value to the silent majority who didn't contribute. The leaders and the active members may have convinced themselves that everyone in the group "identified" with their anxieties and concerns, thus receiving something of value from the session despite little participation. This illusion is not uncommon in therapy. The unpleasant truth is that those who appear bored to death in group session are usually bored to death. Those who seem frustrated often feel exactly that way. The group *splits*, without open conflict.

When the leaders did assert themselves, it wasn't to heal the breach between the Actives and the Passives. Instead they indulged in what we call "one-to-one therapy in groups," negating the value of the group experience and further widening the gap between Actives and Passives.

When Albert confronted the group with his intention to terminate, he received negative feedback from Actives and staff alike. We doubt this sprang from concern about Albert's mental health. We think he challenged the value of the group itself. And in a group such as this, that is forbidden. We call such a group "static." It *discourages* change. Its unstated agenda is pretty much as Albert described it – to permit members to stay as they are. Rather than bonding to a process of change, this group bonds negatively to a mode of resistance. It weds itself to inactivity. Such groups do, we suppose, perpetuate their own existence by encouraging dependence. But they permit only the illusion of change.

□   □   □

A static group develops when a mode of resistance is allowed to become the dominant, accepted form of interaction – the norm for that group. Like a sick family, the static group perverts the language and values of therapy to its own ends: Defense mechanisms are perceived as insights, resistance as work, and stasis as change.

But of course, *all* therapy groups feature a certain measure of resistance. Static and work groups both emerge from the same soil: a group struggling with the process of change. Differences emerge as each strives to deal with its own resistance. Below we describe some of the resistant modes any group might experience and any leader might encounter.

THE HELPLESS GROUP: "WE CAN'T POSSIBLY DO IT OURSELVES"

Helpless, or dependent, groups bond negatively around their own powerlessness. Members assume that, as a group, they lack the knowledge, maturity, potency, or insight to address their own difficulties. This assumed helplessness then dictates their interaction.

Helpless groups often devote a great deal of effort to engaging the leader in conversation. Sometimes they'll ask direct questions; if this is unsuccessful, the group might resort to tentative, hesitant discussion while frequently checking the Leader for his or her response to various remarks.

Such groups are often found complaining about how they "haven't been told" what to do in the group. They tend to "forget" instructions just given to them, necessitating more teaching by the designated leader. They claim to be "confused" by any demands or expectations of participation.

They have extreme difficulty setting boundaries on their own members and tend to permit rambling discussion about the weather or about the rising cost of electricity. Failing that, they may sit silently and wait for the leader to take over. In other words, they baffle and bother the therapist to the point where he or she abandons any agenda other than aggressively intervening to direct and control discussion. Unfortunately, this aggressiveness on the part of the leader compounds the problem by firmly cementing the group into a dependent posture.

When a group flounders, unable to decide what to do or how to do it, it is sending a message to a leader: We cannot do this by ourselves. We lack the resources to make use of an hour of therapy. We're not bright enough, or "well" enough, or determined enough. *You have to help us.*

This is tempting to a leader. After all, he or she does understand group process better than anyone else in the group. So why not jump right in and "fix" this struggling group? After all, that's what leaders are for, isn't it?

No, it isn't. Leaders are present to encourage the group to work. They do not exist to do the work for the group. When a leader assumes responsibility for group interaction, he or she also unwittingly assumes responsibility for achieving the goals of the individual members. Success or failure—for the group itself, and *also for the members' recovery*—now falls on his shoulders.

There are two flaws inherent in this situation.

First, group therapy is of value *only* to the extent that group members interact with each other, thus creating a group culture which can positively influence change. A group that depends on the designated leader to develop and sustain interaction is little different from individual therapy with an audience. Second, therapists don't have a cure for alcoholism or drug dependency. They simply give a form of advice. In this, they are little different from an AA sponsor, a minister, a casual friend, the alcoholic's own family, or anybody who advises the alcoholic about his drinking. So no therapist, no matter how skilled, can legitimately assume responsibility for another person's recovery. That would be a fraud. Group therapy is good for alcoholics precisely because it is an opportunity for them to initiate (and take responsibility for) their own recovery. Assumed helplessness on the part of the group flies in the face of this essential truth about treatment. It's no different from a sick alcoholic wandering from "expert" to "expert" seeking a magical cure for his loss of control. It just wastes a lot of time that could be put to better use elsewhere.

Features of "Helpless" Groups

- *Bonding: Negative,* around the belief that the group itself is helpless and must depend on a designated leader.
- *Climate:* The *background* climate in this mode is one of helplessness and hopelessness. The *foreground* climate might be confusion, ignorance, frustration with the group, or "magical thinking."
- *Values:* The emphasis within this group is on the ability to depend on a designated leader or therapist who, it is assumed, will provide the essential information, skills, or direction for the group.

    Comfort is valued over autonomy. Additionally, the group will equate *total time* spent in sessions with work done; little attention will be paid to the *quality* of interaction in the group. Group members might make statements such as, "What do you mean, we're not accomplishing anything? What do you think we've been doing for the last hour?"

Assignment of roles within such a group will have to be by the leader. Groups in this mode would really rather be at a lecture or religious ceremony; members tend to gravitate towards the roles of "student" or "worshiper."

• *Status:* All authority stems from the leader. The group may *resist* the leader's overtures or directions (and often does), but cannot *initiate* activity.

• *Traditions:* None, except as laid down by the leader.

• *Structure:* Again, as set forth by the leader. Helpless groups often experience many structural changes as the leader seeks vainly to get the group to work; of course, the group *cannot* work without giving up its underlying assumption of helplessness.

• *Mentality:* That of a young child.

• *Culture:* A struggle will appear between any members who try to work and the rest of the group, who will resist it.

It's important to remember that the helpless mode is common in the early stages of the development of any group and that groups normally return to this mode when stymied or confronted with some unfamiliar task. A group becomes a "helpless group" only when allowed to adopt this mode permanently, as a primary form of interaction. Then the group is "stuck" in a dependent role and will actively *resist any responsibility* for the direction of leadership of the group. When this happens, *it's always with the cooperation of the leader.*

Process Example: The Helpless Mode

There are six participants and one leader in this group. The session is just beginning. After everyone is seated, there are several moments of silence.

LEADER   Today we're going to discuss the signs and symptoms of addiction that the members of our group have experienced. Who'd like to start?
(More silence)
LEADER   John, how about you? You haven't talked much in

the group so far. What are some of the symptoms of alcoholism that you've experienced?

JOHN   What do you mean?

LEADER   Well, first of all, what brings you here?

JOHN   I had problems with my wife.

LEADER   How did those problems relate to your drinking?

JOHN   I don't think they did.

LEADER   Then how did they cause you to end up here? This is an alcoholism program.

JOHN   She said I had to come.

LEADER   Do you always do what she wants you to do?

JOHN   (grinning) No.

LEADER   Then why did you consent to come here?

JOHN   I had a DWI.

LEADER   That could certainly be a symptom, couldn't it?

JOHN   I don't know about that.

LEADER   How about some of the rest of you? I can't believe that John is the only person in this group who ever got a DWI.

(Group members look at each other, but no one answers.)

LEADER   You won't get much out of treatment unless you talk in these group meetings, you know. How about you, Louise?

LOUISE   I don't know what to talk about.

LEADER   Try talking about the symptoms of alcoholism you've had.

LOUISE   I don't remember what they are.

LEADER   You don't? How long have you been in treatment?

LOUISE   Three or four weeks.

LEADER   Then I'm sure you and your counselor have discussed your drinking. Didn't you talk about the symptoms of alcoholism?

LOUISE   I don't remember.

LEADER   I have a little trouble believing that.

LOUISE   It's true.

LEADER   Mike, what about you?

MIKE   What about me what?

LEADER   Look, this is like pulling teeth. You've all been in

the program for at least a week, and you've all been in
groups, and you've all been to classes on addiction. Why is
everybody so reluctant to talk?

LOUISE   Well, I told you I don't know what to say in these
groups. I'm not a counselor. I'm not trained.

LEADER   You don't need to be a counselor to talk in groups,
you know.

LOUISE   It just seems to me that you people expect so
much from us.

JOHN   How long does the group last?

LEADER   Why?

JOHN   Just curious.

LEADER   Let's continue, Louise. What's wrong with just
saying whatever is on your mind?

LOUISE   I'm not knowledgeable. I don't know what to say.

LEADER   Do the rest of you feel that way?
(silence)

LOUISE   See? They don't know how to talk about things
either. You have to show us.

LEADER   Just talk about the symptoms of alcoholism
you've experienced. Just as you would with your doctor or
your counselor.

LOUISE   You have to tell us what they are.

LEADER   I suspect you already know.

LOUISE   Well, you're wrong. We don't. We're sorry to disap-
point you. We just aren't very good patients, I guess.

LEADER   OK, Louise. What would help the group to do
better?

LOUISE   Why don't you just teach? We enjoy the classes.

LEADER   Louise, you have a lecture every day. This group is
an opportunity to *use* what you learned in the lecture.

LOUISE   We don't know enough. It's too early.

LEADER   John, are you as uninformed as Louise?

JOHN   I don't know.

LOUISE   I don't understand why you just don't tell us what
to do. It would save a lot of time.

LEADER   Because if I take over, I defeat the purpose of the group. What happens when you leave here? You'll have to talk at AA.

MIKE   Oh.

(silence for several moments)

MIKE   Is it OK to talk about drunk driving tickets?

LEADER   What do *you* think?

MIKE   Well, does anybody know if they take your license away for your second arrest?

JOHN   I don't know. But they're really throwing the book at people now.

MIKE   I don't think that's fair.

JOHN   Neither do I. But I have this one friend who got two DWI's, and they sent him . . .

LEADER   The purpose of this group is to identify the symptoms of alcoholism, not to tell war stories.

LOUISE   See? We don't know what to do. You should be leading us. That's what you get paid to do, isn't it? We try, and then you tell us we're not doing it right. So *you* tell us what to talk about.

LEADER   Louise, I thought we'd cleared this up . . .

THE HOSTILE MODE:
"IT'S A JUNGLE IN HERE."

Suppose that, despite the efforts of the members, the designated leader successfully resists assuming total responsibility for the success or failure of the group. What options remain?

Well, group members could decide to take on the responsibility themselves. That would undoubtedly produce the greatest amount of achievement in the shortest period. However, that seems to be too simple a solution for most groups. Instead, they most often choose to get *angry* with the leader.

Hostile groups come in two forms: *active* and *passive*. Actively hostile groups appoint spokespersons – emissaries of group discontent – who then try to pick a fight with the designated leader. If all goes well, the leader will feel guilty about not living up to what the members see as his or her responsibility, and will subsequently give in and resume control of the group, thus thrusting it back into helplessness. Passively hostile groups, on the other hand, indulge in distracting or undermining behavior which sabotages the group as effectively as open conflict.

Following are examples of active and passive hostility.

Active Hostility

The group session had been struggling for about 30 minutes. Discussion had centered on the contention of several members that they were not given adequate information to prepare for the group. The group's stated task—to discuss the problems with alcohol which had led to the members' seeking treatment—was, they insisted, "just rehashing old stuff that we've already been over a thousand times." Some members had been requesting that the leader take over the discussion and become more active in the group, since, as they put it, he was "the only person here qualified to lead."

When the leader pointed out that every group member had extensive and intimate experience with problems caused by drinking, and therefore was capable of discussing it, one member suddenly flared.

"Dammit", he said angrily, "that's a bunch of hogwash. I don't pay good money to come to a group and have a bunch of drunks discuss my personal life with me. *You're* the one who's supposed to know something, and you won't do anything. A fat lot I'm getting out of *this* group."

Another member chimed in. "I totally agree," she said, "What are we paying you for if you won't help us? I don't have any knowledge about alcoholism . . . that's why I'm in this group. You keep saying that I'm responsible for treating my own illness. OK, I agree. So I'm going to drop out of this group so I can handle things the way I always thought I should—by myself."

Then the first speaker turned the leader and glared at him. "Well?" he said, "That's how we all feel. What do you have to say for yourself?"

Passive Hostility

For several sessions, the leader had resisted the group's apparent efforts to place her in an all-knowing "teacher" role. The members had even gone so far as to suggest that the group switch to a lecture format, so that she could "really be of some use" to them.

At the fourth session, three members arrived late and one didn't show at all. During the session, one man went to the bathroom four times. Another got up twice and refilled everyone's coffee cup.

When the leader confronted the group with this behavior one vocal member told her, "Look, we've tried to please you every way we know how, and you never seem satisfied. Why don't you just accept that we don't know how to do this, and take over?"

Features of "Hostile" Groups

- *Bonding: Negative,* around the idea that the group must protect itself from a common enemy – the leader, or the unreasonableness of the task.
- *Climate: Background* climate is primarily anger and low self-esteem. In the foreground, of course, is hostility in either passive or active form.
- *Values:* In one sense, this mode represents an advance from helplessness, since it at least places some value on autonomous function, though chiefly by devaluing the leader. The group still values *total time expended* rather than work done, and is in fact quite prone to useless socializing. Members are not asking themselves whether or not anything is being accomplished as a result of their activity.

Additionally, groups in this mode are prone to creating strict and unworkable rules which cannot be effectively enforced. If lateness is a problem, for example, the group will probably decide to lock the door at precisely the starting time for the session. Of course, this won't solve the problem, since the point of group isn't to *block* members from attending.

Lastly, this group obviously snatches the leader role and

bestows authority on the most vocal or angriest members, who use this authority to prevent work.

- *Status and traditions:* As mentioned, leadership becomes a hostage of the mode. There are no traditions except simple dissatisfaction with and devaluation of the leader.
- *Structure:* Rigid. This group will impose boundaries and rules as *punishments* rather than supports for work. Structure may become more important than any task.
- *Mentality:* This group is not dealing with a disease or with the problems that brought members to treatment. It is engaged in a fight with a designated leader. Consequently, there is considerable displacement onto the leader.
- *Culture:* A struggle develops between any member who wants to treat his or her disease and the majority of the group, which is taking the position that there is no way that members *can* work with their woefully inadequate leader.

Vocal members who have led resistance – we might call them "consultants" – are incapable of initiating positive activity within the group. They can only lead battles against authority or against the task. If and when the leader is successfully immobilized, these consultants will have trouble deciding how to spend the remainder of the session. They may begin fighting among themselves, or turn into tyrannical figures within the group.

Clinicians tend to see certain members of the hostile group as "ringleaders" who agitate others. This is a gross underestimation of the power of the group. Silent or apparently passive members of such groups are really active participants in resistance. Recall that the "purpose" of the hostile mode is to avoid responsibility for work. The struggles of this mode simply camouflage resistance to personal change.

Process Example: Active Hostility

The session that began in the helpless mode now continues, becoming increasingly hostile.

LOUISE   I am getting *so* tired of being told that I should already know what to do when I have said time and time again that I do not know what to do.

MIKE   Right on.

LEADER   Louise, I have trouble believing that after a number of group sessions you still don't have any idea what to talk about in group therapy.

LOUISE   That is *true*. I'm sick and tired of having people tell me I'm not doing what I'm supposed to, when I don't know what that is. I am tired of having to perform up to other people's expectations.

MIKE   Louise is right, man. I mean, you people ask us to talk about things, and then when we do you tell us we're not talking about the right thing. If I say yes, I'm wrong; if I say no, I'm wrong. If you don't like what we talk about, then *you* talk.

LOUISE   You counselors are all the same. You go to school and get a degree and you think you know everything about people. Well, I have news for you. You *don't*.

JOHN   How long does this group last?

LEADER   What about you, John? Do you feel it's unfair to be asked to talk in the group?

JOHN   I don't know. But I *am* a drunk, you know. If I knew anything, I would never have ended up here in the first place.

MIKE   I don't think these counselors know much about anything, either. I don't think our fearless leader knows too much about drugs.

LEADER   But I'm not the one with the problem . . .

LOUISE   There you go! Throwing our problems into our faces! I am not going to sit here and take that kind of abuse!

LEADER   Louise, calm down . . .

JOHN   Well, *this* is a terrific way to spend an hour . . .

Process Example: Passive Hostility

The scene is the same group one day later. Group members are at least five minutes late. The group remains silent for several minutes after everyone is seated.

LEADER   Well, perhaps we ought to talk about what hap-
pened yesterday.
(Silence; no one responds.)
LEADER   Louise, what about you?
LOUISE   I'm not talking.
LEADER   Why not?
LOUISE   I'm just not.
MIKE   She said she isn't talking. Leave her alone, why don't
you?
(silence)
JOHN   Anybody know what time it is?
MIKE   Why don't you buy a watch?
JOHN   Touchy, touchy.
MIKE   Look, I'm going to get coffee. Anybody want some?
LOUISE   That sounds nice. Cream only, please.
MIKE   I thought you liked sweet-and-low.
LOUISE   Oh, yes, that's right. Please. One packet.
JOHN   How about hot tea?
MIKE   All right.
JOHN   Hey, could you also bring a couple of graham crack-
ers?
LEADER   What is this, lunch?
LOUISE   (with heavy sarcasm) Oh, I suppose you want us to
talk about our problems. So you can criticize us.
LEADER   Louise . . .
MIKE   I'll be back in a few minutes.
JOHN   That's a lot to carry. I better go along.
LEADER   This is ridiculous . . .

THE HOPEFUL EXPECTATION MODE:
"SOMETHING GOOD WILL COME FROM THIS."

The group portrayed in Albert's story is a long-term, set-in-
concrete example of the hopeful expectation mode. Instead of
openly rejecting the group or the leader, members bond around
the idea that simple attendance and willingness to discuss
problems will somehow effect behavior change.

Consider the fellow in Albert's group who desired a better
job. He realized that he hated his present position; this is far

from unusual in the workday world. Changing jobs, he believed, might reduce his dissatisfaction. But the thought of applying and interviewing competitively made him nervous. "Suppose I'm not good enough?" he thought, "Suppose I'm not *capable* of anything better. If that's true, I'd rather not *know*." Therefore, his choice became to risk failure and rejection or to stay where he was. Both seemed intolerable. Then he found an alternative: join a therapy group and *talk* about his situation. Once he did so, the group quickly reinforced his passivity by teaching him that there must be some secret buried in his past which, if discovered and "dealt with," could result in restored confidence and a way out of his dilemma.

Hopeful expectation groups are ideal for such purposes. They thrive on talk. They make excuses for inaction.

Features of Hopeful Expectation Groups

* *Bonding: Negative,* around the idea that something or someone will "appear" in the group to save members from painful choices.
* *Climate: Background* climate focuses on feelings of hostility and defeat. *Foreground* climate features hopefulness. There is a real disparity between the group's reluctance to take initiative or make changes and its insistence that things are somehow "getting better."
* *Values:* This mode values dependency on each other and on the leader and values total time expended above quality of work. Members often "pair off" or form "camps" or "factions" within the group. This is perhaps the ultimate "socializing" group and may see its primary function as "support" and "companionship" rather than change. *Roles* within the group are somewhat flexible, and there may be one or two "surrogate leaders" among the members, who dominate discussion and the group's agenda.
* *Status:* Informal.
* *Tradition:* Avoiding work is perfectly acceptable, as long as therapeutic-type interactions occur. This group is long on form and short on content.
* *Mentality:* "Help is on the way."

• *Culture:* A struggle will emerge between group members who
want to progress and those who are dedicated to maintaining
stasis. Some members will stay in this group entirely too
long, while others will drop out before getting any work done.
Designated leaders may ally with long-time members or
"trustees"; they also value dependency over work.

While helpless and hostile modes tend to proliferate in the
early stages of a group, the hopeful expectation mode lends
itself to the kind of chronic stasis experienced by Albert's
group. Morale among members may be relatively high, despite
the lack of measurable progress. Dominant or active members
tend to be nonworkers rather than workers, and with the compliance of the designated leaders these "Actives" may establish
a system of values which supports their own reluctance to
change.

Underlying the pointless, purposeless, and repetitive "therapeutic interactions" of the hopeful expectation group is the
assumption that, somehow, talk is action. This isn't true. *Action* is action. Talk is talk.

Process Example: Hopeful Expectation Mode

We look in on the same group three days later. Two members
of the group are missing.

LOUISE   I'd like to begin, if you don't mind. I just want to
     apologize for my outburst of a few days ago, and for
     missing the last two groups. I was upset, but I had a
     wonderful talk with my therapist, and she showed me that
     you were only trying to help me.
LEADER   All right, Louise, but you don't really have to
     apologize . . .
LOUISE   No, I want to. I was wrong to lose my temper.
MIKE   I guess I owe you an apology, too. I was quick on the
     trigger. I'm that kind of guy.
LEADER   I'm not so awful, huh?
MIKE   No.
JOHN   This group is going great. We've already used up 15
     minutes.

LEADER   I notice two members are missing.

LOUISE   Yes, they left last night.

LEADER   Why?

LOUISE   Well, they weren't willing to forgive you for the last few days of group. They were pretty upset. I can understand it, though I think they were wrong to go. I believe the group is really helping.

MIKE   They just wanted to drink is all. They would have left anyway.

LEADER   Well, that's too bad. Still, it's good the two of you stayed.

MIKE   We want to get well.

LOUISE   I feel that if we just keep coming to the group, we'll get better. Sometimes I'm not ready to work on my problems, it's a bad day or something, but just coming here seems to help. I plan to go to aftercare, too, so I hope I'll get to come back to see you all.

MIKE   We can ride together.

LOUISE   That would be fun. Where do you live?

MIKE   Coffeeville.

LOUISE   Oh, I'm right down the road . . .

LEADER   Perhaps we'd better use this time to work on some issues. After all, you and Mike are leaving in a day or two.

LOUISE   Of course, you're right.

LEADER   Anybody have anything in particular to discuss?

LOUISE   Well I'd like to discuss my relationship with my husband. He's a heavy drinker. When I came in, I thought I'd have to separate from him if I wanted to stay sober. But now I see that I don't really have to do that. I can stay sober, and be patient, and go to Alanon, and maybe he will change.

JOHN   God, that sounds rough. How do you know you won't get drunk?

LOUISE   I made up my mind not to. I don't have any desire for alcohol.

JOHN   Yeah, but you will, when you get back in that environment.

LOUISE   John, look, you take care of your problems, and I'll take care of mine.

JOHN   OK, OK, don't be so touchy . . .

LEADER   I think John has a point, Louise. That sounds like
a rough way to get sober, living with a drinking alcoholic.

LOUISE   There you go again, criticizing my decisions. First
you tell me to trust my feelings, then you turn around and
tell me to change the only decision I finally make. . . .

LEADER   I'm not telling you to do anything. It's your
decision. But it does sound risky.

MIKE   I don't see why. I plan to hang around all my old
friends, and they hang out in bars. I'm not giving them up.
They're my friends.

JOHN   Wow, I couldn't do that.

MIKE   Well, you're not me.

JOHN   Whew. What a touchy bunch. Only 30 minutes to go.

LEADER   I think there's a valid issue here. How seriously
could you want sobriety if you're not willing to give up your
drinking environment?

LOUISE   Look, we told you what we're going to do. Are you
saying you won't let us come back to the group unless we
do what you want us to?

LEADER   Of course not.

LOUISE   Then I'm just going to go home and come to the
group and hope for the best. I've thought it through and I
just can't do anything else right now.

MIKE   I'm with you.

LEADER   Well, as I said, It's your decision. But I hope you
are as strong as you think you are.

LOUISE   So do I. But I know I have the group, and it's like
they say at AA, "keep coming back." That's what I plan to
do.

MIKE   Me, too.

JOHN   When does the group end?

LEADER   4 o'clock, John.

In the next chapter, we'll review the characteristics of that
all-too-rare creature, the working group. Then we'll discuss the
role of the leader in turning resistance into work.

CHAPTER 4

THE WORK MODE
AND THE
WORKING GROUP

WORK GROWS OUT of nonwork. We've never in all our years seen a group that works from its inception. Progress towards work usually means that the group has at some point struggled through helpless or hostile stages and still on occasion flirts with those modes. But, in fact, the work mode makes its initial appearance very *early,* perhaps when the group seems most lost or resistant. If it can be identified and nurtured, the work mode will become the *dominant* form of interaction within the group. When it does, we say it is a "working group."

CHARACTERISTICS OF THE WORK MODE

Bonding

In the work mode the group bonds *positively* around the task. For this to occur, of course, the group must have been given (or selected) an appropriate task. In addictions, this task must reflect the *goals of treatment*: those supposedly desired objectives which brought the members to the group in the first place. A task is seen as an opportunity rather than an obligation; something that reflects the group's need rather than an external standard.

Climate

One of the best ways to recognize this mode is through a generalized (though unmistakable) change in climate. When an addictions treatment group is working, the *background* climate reflects *fear of the disease*. Members act as if they have an illness which deserves their full attention. That fear is one major motive for attending the group, as well as for sticking with the group while it learns to work and changing behavior outside the group.

Let's stop to compare interactions in resistant and working modes. The following exchange takes place when the group members are resisting change.

BUCK   So why are you here?

TAMMY   I was fighting a lot with my husband, and when I got a DWI, he used it to force me into this program.

BUCK   That's rough. But I had a couple of DWI's myself, and my lawyer got me off.

TAMMY   Well, that wasn't all. I was drinking a lot. But it was something I could have taken care of myself, if people would have left me alone.

HARRY   Everybody says that, but it's just promises. I tried to quit drinking for ten years, and I don't think I ever made it more than a few months.

TAMMY   Well, that doesn't mean I couldn't have quit. You're not me.

BUCK   Yeah, I was off for a year once, back when I was younger. Quit on my own. Wish I hadn't started back up again.

TAMMY   (to Harry) So you see, there's my point. You just need the right set of circumstances.

Now, compare that to this exchange as the group begins to work:

BUCK   Yeah, I was off for a year once, back when I was younger. Quit on my own. Wish I hadn't started back up again.

RALPH   So why did you?

BUCK   Broke up with my woman.

HARRY   So that's what I'm saying: it's always something.
Maybe you're sober a week, maybe a year, even ten years.
But as long as it's you alone, it's only a matter of time.

TAMMY   You can say that about yourself, but I don't see
how you can say that about me. You hardly know me.

MARTHA   He can say it about you because you're an alcoholic. That's what alcoholics do, whether they want to or not. I
never wanted to get drunk – I just wanted to feel better, for
a little while. But I couldn't stop myself with one drink – or
even with one night of drinking.

HARRY   Me either. But look at it this way, Tammy: How
long have you been trying to handle this on your own? And
how much success have you had? And how much more
research do you want to do?

With this in the background, the *foreground* climate is usually a fear of not working, as in, "If we don't get to Work, we
might well get drunk again, and who's to say we'll survive
another binge?"

Here is another example of the resistant mode:

DANIEL   Look, I can't talk tonight. I've had a terrible week,
and I just can't stand to think about this anymore.

RICARDO   Don't you think you should tell us about it? I
mean, so you don't just have to handle it all by yourself?

DANIEL   What could you do about it?

LOIS   You could express your feelings. It would make you
feel better.

DANIEL   I think it would just make me anxious.

LOIS   Well, you could start talking, and then if you got
anxious, you could stop.

RICARDO   Yeah, you wouldn't have to do anything except
talk. That's what we're here for: to feel better. You just talk
as long as it's comfortable. Then stop whenever you want.

In the work mode the group handles Daniel's evasiveness
differently:

DANIEL   Look, I can't talk anymore. I've had a terrible week, and I just can't stand to think about this anymore.

RICARDO   Don't you think you should tell us about it? I mean, so you don't just have to handle it all by yourself?

DANIEL   What could you do about it?

LOIS   I don't know. We don't know what the problem is. Why don't you tell us?

DANIEL   I think it would just make me anxious.

RICARDO   I think you're already pretty anxious. Probably because you're trying to handle this whole problem by yourself. That's how you get in trouble.

LOIS   That's true. That's what I do – take everything on my shoulders and then fall apart when it overwhelms me.

DANIEL   I feel like I'll fall apart if I talk about it.

LOIS   I think you'll fall apart if you don't. And do you really need to get drunk again?

DANIEL   That is the last thing I need at this point in my life. That would just about ruin my last chance at everything.

RICARDO   So just start at the beginning, and tell us what happened.

Morale in such groups is *high*, despite the fact that members might be experiencing some anxiety. When a group which has been struggling in the hostile or helpless modes breaks through into work, you'll see an almost tangible change in the tenor of discussion. Members will begin to sense that at last they are "getting somewhere" and that they have, in fact, begun to *find their own way* into recovery.

Values

The work mode values autonomy over dependence. People not only want to recover from their disease, but also *want to learn how to treat themselves.* They are suspicious of relying on authority figures, such as a designated leader. They want *information* about addiction and how to treat it, but they don't want their recovery to be dependent on another person. People in work groups continue to want strokes from the leader, however, for their work. As far as time invested, work groups clearly value *quality of interaction* rather than total time in group sessions.

Again, let us look at an exchange in the resistant and work mode, starting with the former:

JEREMY   Well, I don't know how you can say I don't try hard enough to get better—I've been to every group for three months. I've sacrificed a lot to get here.

VINCE   We're not saying you haven't gotten anything out of the group—just that you hardly ever say anything.

JEREMY   I talk. Maybe not as much as you, but when I have something to say, I say it.

VINCE   But the point is, are you getting enough so you can stay sober after you stop coming to the group?

JEREMY   Look, I did my part. The judge told me to come, and I came. I didn't want to, but I did it. I didn't like the group sometimes. Sometimes I thought it was pretty good. But I came.

VINCE   Well, I guess we'd have to give you credit for that, at least.

JEREMY   Damn straight.

In the work mode Jeremy's excuses are not accepted:

JEREMY   Look, I did my part. The judge told me to come, and I came. I didn't want to, but I did it. I didn't like the group sometimes. Sometimes I thought it was pretty good. But I came.

NADINE   This isn't a movie, Jeremy. You sound like you think we're supposed to entertain you for a couple of hours.

VINCE   You're here in body but not in mind, friend.

JEREMY   I listen to everything that's said.

NADINE   And respond to nothing. See, the reality is that you could leave here, start drinking again, and get another DWI.

JEREMY   No way. I made a promise I will never again drive

after six p.m. I'm giving the keys to my wife as soon as I
get home from work.
VINCE   Is that an alcoholic for you? Faced with a choice
between giving up drinking and giving up driving, he
decides to quit driving his own car.

Work groups do *not* value socializing during the group.
Members may be close friends outside, but they do not chat
within the boundaries of the session. *Roles* are flexible; group
members pass "leadership" around according to skill and inclination. However, they are strict about the boundaries of their
meeting.

Traditions

The group establishes its own traditions. Work groups are
always telling new members, "This is the way we do it around
here." Predominantly working groups will carry their traditions
with them through some amazing changes in location, membership, and designated leaders.

Structure

Work groups, despite a superficial appearance of rigidity in
some cases, are flexible *when change is necessary*. Nonwork
groups will collapse in the face of external changes or challenges; work groups will adapt.

Mentality

In a work group, *only* work is acceptable.

Culture

The work of the group – whatever it may be – continues even
when individual members attempt to disrupt it.

In an *advanced* stage, a "working group" will show a real cooperative spirit. Members will bond not only around the task and the goals of treatment, but also around each other.

The background climate of such an advanced group will feature less fear of the disease and more emphasis on the shared experience of increased self-worth which comes from *success*. In the foreground, the members will seem *proud of their group*.

Values, in this advanced stage, will continue to be on *autonomy* (the designated leader will be seen as a "consultant" only), *quality of interaction,* and *protection of the task*.

Roles will be internalized. Status is informal; whoever has the skill or knowledge gets the "job." Traditions in such a group will be established to an extreme degree, with the designated leaders as much bound by the group's traditions as the members.

The mentality of such a group is one of understanding. Members now know *why* they invest energy in the work of the group. They are clear as to its benefits.

And in terms of culture, work has become the expected norm. Disruption is not tolerated.

PROCESS EXAMPLE: WORK MODE

Let us look in again on our hypothetical group from Chapter 3. John has just asked for the time once again.

MIKE   I wish you'd stop asking that stupid question, John. What do you think, that you're supposed to just sit here and wait for the group to end? You think it's just a matter of sitting in one place for an hour?

JOHN   Well, that's what *you* think.

MIKE   What are you talking about?

JOHN   You and Louise sit here and talk about how you just spent three weeks in a program for alcoholism and you're going to go right out and hang around with your friends who are still drinking, and you're going to be able to stay sober because you come to this group.

LOUISE   So what is wrong with that?

JOHN   It's a load of hooey. I've been in this group with you,
and most of the time nothing happens at all. Sure, I count
the minutes, but you guys might as well be punching in
and out on a time clock. I mean, you show up, but you don't
accomplish anything.

LOUISE   Yes, we do. I resent that.

JOHN   Well, you push the leader around, I suppose.

LOUISE   I do not!

JOHN   You do. I can't figure out why he lets you do it. Tell
me one thing – just one thing – that has changed as a result
of being in this group.

LOUISE   I quit drinking.

JOHN   Big deal. You could have done that in a Holiday Inn
with some pills from your shrink.

ALICE   John's right. This is my third group, but even I can
see that you guys are just playing games.

LOUISE   That's your opinion.

MIKE   Right on. It's just an opinion. It's not the Gospel.
John isn't an expert on you, Louise. He doesn't know you.

JOHN   I know her well enough. Louise, is this the first time
you've been through a treatment program?

MIKE   She doesn't have to tell you that.

JOHN   Why hide it? How about you, Mike? Is this your first
trip?

ALICE   Answer the question.

MIKE   No, it isn't my first trip. Though I don't see what
that has to do with anything.

JOHN   When did you leave the hospital?

MIKE   About a year ago.

JOHN   How about you, Louise?

LOUISE   I was in here six months ago.

JOHN   How long after you left did you start drinking again?

LOUISE   A couple of months.

ALICE   Boy, this program really did *you* a lot of good.

LOUISE   What concern is it of yours?

ALICE   Hey, none whatsoever. But it looks to me like you're
setting yourself up for a return engagement in a few
months.

LOUISE   You don't know that.
LEADER   I think she has a point, Louise.
LOUISE   (angrily) There you are, criticizing me again.
LEADER   It isn't criticism. I'm just being honest with you.
LOUISE   (starts to cry)
ALICE   Oops, watch your cigarettes everybody, here comes
the flood. . . .
MIKE   (to leader) Now see what you did?
JOHN   Oh, Mike, why don't you knock it off? She doesn't
need you to protect her. Why don't you stop enabling her?
Maybe you'll both be better off.
ALICE   I couldn't have said it better myself.
MIKE   We're trying to get sober together, and you. . . .
ALICE   Hey, no offense, but you guys don't know how to get
sober separately, so I don't know how you plan to get sober
together. You're no help to each other.
JOHN   What about some of the rest of you in this group?
Why don't we let you all talk for a while? I mean, you're
here to get well as much as we are, right?

There's one more thing to remember: Where the three modes
of resistance reinforce and perpetuate themselves, the work
mode is *always transient*. Staying in the helpless, hostile, or
hopeful expectation mode is easy. Work, on the other hand,
requires some degree of knowledge and persistence, and almost
always produces a certain level of anxiety, however harmless.
So the group's natural tendency is to slip in and out of various
modes, perhaps spending no more than 15 to 20 minutes at a
time in any given one. The practical advantage is that even the
most resistant group will probably generate small "windows" of
work that can be recognized and encouraged.
    Someone once asked us why, since work requires so little
intervention from a trained facilitator, we have a leader in the
group. The answer is that no group, however wondrous, works
all the time. Thus the leader's job is to nurture the appearance
of the work mode.

CHAPTER 5

EXERCISES IN GROUP PROCESS

NOW WE'RE READY to practice the most important of all leadership skills: learning to recognize group process *as it happens*.

Keep in mind that we are studying *groups*, rather than individuals. It's easy to let yourself be distracted by the behavior of a member, or even a leader, while the really important shifts in mode occur unnoticed. To process groups effectively, we have to view all individual behavior against a background of developing group process.

The remainder of this section is devoted to edited transcripts of seven addictions treatment groups. We've tried to include a broad range of settings: detox groups, inpatient treatment groups, multiple family therapy groups, aftercare groups, outpatient groups, etc. You will find examples of good and bad leadership in good and bad sessions. Again, don't be distracted by the setting: The same shifts in mode that occur in a group full of 10-day-sober alcoholics will occur in a sophisticated family session.

After each example, we have provided space for you to enter your own process notes. Refer back to the sections on process and terminology if necessary, until you are familiar with the material. Answer the questions provided as guidelines: How does the group bond? What shifts in mode occur? What alternative interventions might have been initiated? What is the dominant mode of this group? Its mentality? Its values? How does it assign roles? Delegate authority? And so on.

Then, after you've made your own observations, compare them with ours.

By the time you've completed the exercises, you should have a working familiarity with the terminology of group process as we see it. The ensuing chapters will add suggestions on how to structure and to lead addictions groups so as to maximize the amount of work done.

GROUP PROCESS EXERCISE #1: DETOX GROUP

This group takes place in a facility for detoxifying alcoholics and addicts. There are seven members and one leader. All members are less than ten days from their last drink or drug use.

> All members are seated. After 15 or 10 seconds of silence, Dale speaks.

DALE   Well, isn't anyone going to say something? Are we just going to sit here like bumps on a log?

RUBY   I thought the leader was supposed to start.

(All eyes go to leader.)

LEADER   What would you all like to discuss today?

DALE   I don't mean to be rude, but why do you counselors always answer a question with a question?

LEADER   Do we?

DALE   Yes, you do. And it gets very irritating.

RUBY   Dale, I think you're being petty.

DALE   I'm sorry, but it gets on my nerves.

(Another brief silence ensues. Then Harry speaks.)

HARRY   Well, I've got something. I've just about made up my mind to go home. When I got here a couple of days ago, I was really mad at my wife. She was just nagging me to death, and it was either come here or do something I'd regret. But last night, we had a great talk. We really talked for the first time in years. So that problem is over. And I'm thinking now that if I don't get back to work, I might get fired. So I think I better not stay any longer. I better get back to work.

RUBY   Are you sure? You looked pretty sick yesterday.

HARRY   Naw, I wasn't that sick. I had a few pills, and it fixed me right up. I was never that sick in the first place.

FRANK   Sounds like you're looking for an excuse to leave.

BEN   Now how would *you* know that? I think he's perfectly reasonable. He wants to get back to work. We can't all take time off, you know.

FRANK   But suppose he starts drinking again?

BEN   Well, *you* don't know that's going to happen. I think you ought to have a little faith in people.

FRANK   What does faith have to do with it? We're talking about alcoholism.

LEADER   Maybe this is a good time to get some participation from some other members of the group. How do the rest of you feel about Harry's plans for leaving the hospital?

BEN   Well, I think I've made my opinion clear. Harry knows what is best for him. We ought to let him run his own life. He has a right to go home if he thinks that's best.

FRANK   Nobody's questioning Harry's *right* to go. We're questioning whether or not he's *ready* to leave.

DALE   I don't understand. What would make him *not* ready to go?

FRANK   For one thing, he might want to learn something about alcoholism.

DALE   What's there to learn? We all know we're alcoholics. We know we shouldn't drink. What else is there?

HARRY   That's right. To me, I can stay sober better at home than I can here. It doesn't mean anything to be sober in a controlled environment like this. The question is: Can you stay sober at home, with all the pressure?

FRANK   So how do you know you won't drink when you get under pressure?

HARRY   Look, you just don't know me. I'm a strong-willed guy. I quit smoking five years ago. Just made up my mind, and never touched a cigarette again. I can do the same with booze.

　　See, to me, being here makes it hard to not think about liquor. It's all anybody talks about. At home, my wife is a teetotaler. She'll keep me sober. You should see how much she hates alcohol. I promised her last night I'd never touch another drop.

FRANK   I've made a lot of promises like that. Broke them all.

HARRY   Well, that's *you*.

LEADER   Frank is right; alcoholics break promises about drinking. But what about some of the rest of you? What's your reaction to Harry's plan?

TOM   I'm just listening.

LEADER   You don't have any reaction?

TOM   Noooo . . . say, can I go get a cup of coffee?

LEADER   Is there some reason you don't want to share your feelings with this group?

TOM   Well, I just don't see how this all relates to me. I ain't married.

LEADER   Don't you have a drinking problem?

TOM   Drinking? Oh sure, but Harry's talking about his wife. I don't have any problems with my wife.

LEADER   Don't you think the two problems are related?

TOM   Not necessarily. I mean, it seems to me that Harry has solved his drinking problem. He said he quit, and he sounds like he really means it. So whether or not he goes home to his wife doesn't make a lot of difference. He's not gonna drink no matter what. So the question is: Should he go home or stay here? Drinking has nothing to do with it. And like I said, that doesn't relate to me. I don't have wife problems.

LEADER   You never had problems in your marriage?

TOM   Oh sure, I *used* to, but she left. So that problem is solved. Now it's just the alcohol gives me trouble.

LEADER   Well, tell us about the drinking.

TOM   We ain't finished with Harry.

LEADER   That's OK, we'll get back to Harry. Tell us about yourself. What are your feelings about being here?

TOM   Well . . . Harry's a man. And I'm a man. And when you're a man, you give your word, you have to stick to it. That's what a man does. If you don't do that, you ain't a man. Not to me, anyway.

LEADER   So if Harry makes up his mind not to drink, that's all there is to it, right?

TOM   Absolutely. Therapy don't got nothing to do with it. He's just got to make up his mind. And he already did that.

HARRY   And I meant what I said.

RUBY   Didn't you ever promise to stay sober, and then go ahead and drink? I have.

HARRY   I never did. I never made up my mind before. Oh, I promised people I wouldn't drink and then went ahead and drank, but that was because I never really wanted to stop my own self. I just did it for them.

TOM   Well, then you are on the right road now. If you really want it, you can do it. But if you don't really want it, ain't no program gonna give you the desire. You have to have the desire in your own mind. You either want it or you don't.

HARRY   You are 100% right, friend.

TOM   I'll tell you what gets me. It ain't the booze. It's the loneliness. I'd give up drinking but the loneliness gets to me.

HARRY   Hey, I'll tell you what. After you get out, you come over and visit me. We'll play cards. We'll even go over to a triple A meeting.

FRANK   If you don't get drunk together first.

HARRY   (angrily) DAMN IT! You are so damn negative! Who asked you to put in your two cents? You make me feel like just chucking the whole thing and going and getting me a drink!

LEADER   Let's try to keep calm . . .

HARRY   Well, who made him president of AA, anyway? Looks to me like he's as big a drunk as anybody here.

FRANK   No argument. But you act like I'm attacking you or something.

LEADER   OK, fellows, let's see if we can't get . . .

HARRY   You ARE attacking me. It's people like you who are always going around criticizing people, you're the reason people drink in this world. If there were fewer people like you, there'd be fewer alcoholics, you can guarantee that.

FRANK   Need I remind you that I wound up here, too?

LEADER   Let's talk about something more relevant . . .

BEN   This *is* relevant. Can I ask you a question?

LEADER   Of course.

BEN   Are you personally an alcoholic?

LEADER   I don't see the relevance . . .

DALE   Answer him. I'd like to know.

LEADER   No, as a matter of fact, I'm not.

BEN   I knew it.

DALE   He has a point. How did you get into this field? I thought all the counselors were recovering alcoholics.

LEADER   Some are, but not all of us.

TOM   That's why you can't understand Harry, then. If you were an alcoholic, you'd know that once he makes up his mind, that's it. He's done with alcohol. He's a man.

DALE   That sounds too simple, but there is a point there. If Harry doesn't really want to quit drinking, then therapy won't make him want to. And if he does want to quit, then what good is the therapy?

LEADER   I think that's an oversimplification.

TOM   That's because you ain't an alcoholic. That's the problem. It ain't that Harry don't understand. It's you that don't understand.

BEN   How did you get into this counseling job, anyway? I bet you have a college degree in counseling, right?

LEADER   I do, but the real issue . . .

HARRY   We thought you were a social worker type. We talked about you.

TOM   I don't got no degree. But I know about booze all right. If you done booze, you know about it. If you ain't done it, you can't talk about it.

HARRY   Amen, brother.

LEADER   I don't agree . . .

TOM   You ever been to a college where they teach you how to drink?

LEADER   No, but . . .

TOM   Me, neither. That's my point. You don't learn nothing about drinking in college.

HARRY   This guy (referring to leader) probably just smoked
grass.

DALE   So what? I smoked grass.

HARRY   Yeah, but you grew out of it.

DALE   No, I *still* like it . . .

TOM   (to leader): Look here, do you know the difference
between a gin fizz and a vodka collins?

LEADER   I can't for the life of me see what that has to
do . . .

BEN   Do you drink?

LEADER   That's not important.

BEN   You're avoiding the question.

LEADER   How do you mean that?

DALE   See? It's incredible. Always answers with a question.

FRANK   This group is what's incredible. Here we are talking
about the one person in this group who *doesn't* have a
drinking problem. That's really helping us a lot.

HARRY   What are you, the junior assistant trainee counselor?

FRANK   What are you, a professional moron?

LEADER   Now let's put a stop to this right now. I think
there are some legitimate issues here. Harry is thinking
about leaving the program. I hear his feelings, but I don't
agree with his decision. But I also hear an undercurrent of
"macho" talk. I wonder if this insistence on getting sober
without help is just part of the John Wayne syndrome. You
know: too tough to show feelings, cry, ask for help.

HARRY   (to Tom) What is he talking about?

BEN   Sounds like one of them TV talk show host faggots.

RUBY   You two are disgusting.

(Tom and Harry chuckle along with Ben).

DALE   I think he has a point. I mean, I feel a lot of resentment at not being able to express my feelings in society. I
feel a lot of pressure to hide my real emotions. I *want* to be
open, but I am just not permitted to be in this society.
When I drink, I get the confidence to say what I feel no
matter what anyone thinks.

HARRY   You seem pretty confident to me.

BEN   Maybe he just needs a talk show of his own.

DALE   Up yours.

FRANK   This is stupid. I want you all to know, if you
care, that this is the most worthless hour I've ever
spent. I'm starting to wonder why I stay here. At least if I
went to an AA meeting, I might hear something of
interest.

HARRY   Are you saying I don't know what I'm talking
about?

FRANK   I'm saying I don't know how you figure out which
side of bed to get out of in the morning.

RUBY   Stop it, both of you. Now I'm so upset *I* feel like
leaving this program.

DALE   Me too. But my wife wouldn't take me back.

LEADER   Sounds like we've really lost our way.

FRANK   No kidding. I feel really depressed.

HARRY   I'm definitely leaving.

TOM   Just keep your mind firm. If you let your mind
wander, you're in trouble. So just keep real busy. Get a
hobby or something.

HARRY   Right. And I'll get to the AA's, you'll see.

TOM   Now I don't hold with those AA's. If you're a man, you
don't need them. Maybe women need them, I don't know.
But they're just a crutch. If you're a man, you don't need no
crutch. And if you ain't a man, ain't no AA gonna turn you
into one. So I don't hold with the AA's.

HARRY   You know, *you* ought to be the counselor. You make
more sense.

TOM   Well, I don't have education, but I know alcohol.

Bonding: _____

_____

Climate: _____

_____

Values: _____

_____

_____

Status and traditions, structure: _____

_____

_____

Mentality: _____

_____

Culture: _____

_____

Dominant mode: _____

_____

Other modes during session: _____

_____

_____

Discussion

This is an easy one. The group moves quickly from helplessness into a mode of active hostility and remains there for the
remainder of the session.

• *Bonding:* Negative, around the idea that the group is worthless and the leader is no good.

- *Climate:* Foreground is active resistance to the ostensible purpose of the group; background climate is one of cynicism about the value of any form of treatment in assisting recovery. The group does not consider alcoholism a disease and treats it as a problem of personal choice, despite the fact that this group most likely takes place in an acute hospital setting.
- *Values:* The group makes a point of devaluing the leader, the group itself, and any work done by individual members. Some group members place considerable emphasis on the primacy of willpower, again despite the fact that their presence in the group is an indication that their efforts to control their problem without help have been unsuccessful.
- *Status:* As in most hostile groups, leadership is taken away from the designated leader and assigned to his most vocal critics, Harry and Ben. Their criticism becomes quite personal and cruel, despite the fact that they hardly know the leader and he has made no criticism of them. Tom, the most toxic or confused group member, becomes a "figurehead." This also is characteristic of hostile groups: They frequently elevate to the status of leader someone who is completely unable to fulfill the function.
- *Mentality:* "Treatment is a waste of time, and we might as well all go home."
- *Culture:* A struggle between any member who wants to work (e.g., Frank) and the dominant resistance of the group. If any work is done, the group will have to relinquish its assumption that treatment is valueless. This means that Harry, Ben, et al. will have to consent to treatment they do not want. Therefore, they attack and devalue any workers, just as they did the leader.

By the end of this group session, virtually everyone is ready to sign out of the program against the advice of the counselors.

Alternative Interventions

This group suffers from lack of leadership. In fact, almost any intervention would have produced better results than those used by the leader in this group.

We certainly would have recommended that this leader give the group members a task directing them towards examination of their own behavior rather than that of the leader. After all, who is sick here? As Frank points out, the group members devote attention to the one person in the group who *doesn't* need help, while ignoring their own glaring problems.

It would have been easy for the leader to answer Dale's original challenge ("Do you always answer a question with a question?") by reminding Dale that the purpose of the group was to take a hard look at Dale's drinking, not at the communication style of the leader. This would have redirected the group towards the need to treat alcoholism.

In the same fashion, the leader might well have intervened when Ben first rescued Harry from Frank's appropriate questioning. Or perhaps the leader could have explained that there really *was* something to learn about alcoholism that Harry and Ben didn't know – that it's a disease, for example.

GROUP PROCESS EXERCISE #2:
STEP DISCUSSION GROUP

One of the most widely used formats in alcoholism treatment, the step discussion group focuses on one or more of the Twelve Steps of Alcoholics or Narcotics Anonymous. A given step becomes the topic of discussion, as in an AA Step Meeting. This topic may be abandoned as other "issues" present themselves to the group, and the session may finish on a topic quite different from the one on which it began.

This particular session occurs in an outpatient group which has met for several months. There are eight members and one leader.

For reference, the third step discussed in this example reads as follows: "Made a decision to turn our will and our lives over to the care of God *as we understood Him.*"

LEADER   You all recall our earlier discussions of the Twelve
                 Steps and their role in treatment. We've been over the
                 terms and the meaning of the "Higher Power" in the AA

vocabulary. Today, I think we should move on to a discussion of the third step in particular. Who'd like to open the discussion?

MARY   You know, I don't mean to interrupt, but I just have to tell you that I think you are a terrific leader. You always seem to know just the right topic to get the group off on the right foot. Just last night I was telling my husband what a great counselor you are.

LEADER   Well, Mary, thanks for the strokes, but . . .

MARY   No, I'm sincere. I really do think you're just super.

LEADER   Thank you again. But I think we'd best get to our topic, the third step. Would someone like to tell us what the step says?

MARY   I can. The third step is my favorite, because it tells you how when you have a problem you don't have to get down, because God will help you with it, no matter what it is. God will walk with you. You don't have to walk alone.

I like it much better than the eighth step, which just makes you feel guilty. I don't feel guilty about anything. And I think that step is designed to bring out guilt, which is what you don't need, not with all your other problems. I need to feel better about myself, not worse. The eighth step makes you feel worse.

LEADER   Mary, before we look at the eighth step, I think we ought to look at the third. But Ted, I can't help noticing you look very worried about something. Am I right? How were things at home last week? Can you share with us?

TED   How were things at home? I thought we were on the third step.

LEADER   We are, but perhaps we can link them together. How, for example, would you go about turning your will and your life over to God in terms of your marital situation?

TED   Hey, I'd be glad to turn my will and my wife over to God, if He'll take 'em.

MARY   *Life*, Ted. Not *wife*.

TED   Oh, sorry. My mistake.

LEADER   Ted, I've seen you joke a lot in group. Do you by any chance use jokes to cover up some nervousness?

TED   Gee . . . all my life I've been told I have a great sense
of humor.

LEADER   You do, Ted. But I wonder if you don't sometimes use it to cover up feelings that are uncomfortable for
you.

TED   Well, I don't see how you could say that. I mean, what
makes you think I'm denying anything? Maybe I don't
have anything to deny. Maybe nothing really happened at
home this week. Did you ever stop to think that maybe
there's just nothing to talk about? It doesn't always have to
be denial, you know.

MARY   Well, something sure as heck went on at *my* house
this week. My husband brought up the idea that he wants
to separate. Can you believe the nerve of him? After all
we've been through, and all the years I put up with him . . .
(starts to cry).

I'm sorry, I can't help it, I get so upset. . . .

TED   I'm sure glad Mary is in our group. She always has a
problem to talk about.

MARY   You of all people should understand how I feel . . .

TED   Mary, if you were really working the third step like you
say, you wouldn't have this problem. You'd have turned it
over to God. Isn't that right?

LEADER   That's one interpretation of the step. But before
we go on, what about you, Bob? You look to me like you
have something you want to say. What's your reaction to
the third step?

BOB   Uh . . . which one is the third?

TED   "Made a decision to turn our will and our lives over to
the care of God *as we understood Him.*"

BOB   I can't help Mary with this step because . . . I don't
believe in God.

LEADER   But we discussed that for an hour last week. We
talked about how you can substitute your own idea of a
Higher Power for a traditional Christian God.

BOB   Maybe *you* can do that. But that's not what the step
says. I read it. It says God, right there in black and
white.

MARY   Oh, do we have to discuss this again? We've been all
over this a hundred times.

TED   Yeah, this is even worse than hearing about Mary's
problems with her husband.

(brief silence)

BOB   Well, I don't know if this is off the subject, but I really
came here to tell you all that this is my last night in the
group. I'm dropping out.

(another silence)

I want to thank all of you for your help, but I think I was
really misdiagnosed. I found out this week I'm not an
alcoholic.

MARY   Bob, we went all through this. Are you going to tell
us that you've gone back to denying you're alcoholic again?

BOB   Mary, I am not denying anything. I never admitted I
was an alcoholic. I never said, "I am an alcoholic," to anyone
in this group. So I'm not going back on it. I never committed myself.

But I've always suspected that I wasn't an alcoholic, and
this week I found out for sure I'm not. I have proof.

(more silence)

LEADER   Why don't you share this proof with the group, Bob.

BOB   Well, Tuesday night after group I stopped off in a bar
to buy cigarettes. A couple of my old buddies were there, so
I sat down and had a club soda just to be sociable. Well,
while I was sitting there, I was thinking about what we
talked about in this group, about whether or not I was a
real alcoholic. And I thought; there should be some way to
test it, to know for sure.

So I thought, why don't I have two drinks? If I'm an
alcoholic, I won't be able to stop. Then I'll know that I have
a problem, and I'll get a lot more out of the therapy. As it is
now, I don't even know if I belong here. But if I can stop,
then I'll know my problems with alcohol are over.

So I had two drinks, and I stopped cold. Had no desire
whatsoever. I even sat there, right at the bar, for another
hour, and had no craving for more. Then I went home and
went to sleep.

Well, if I can do that, I'm no alcoholic. And I don't plan
to turn my will over to God or anyone else. I don't need to.
I didn't have another drop until Thursday, and then only
two beers. Still no problem. I couldn't have done that a
month ago. So you people have really helped me.
Now I'm not putting you all down. I don't feel superior.
But it would be dishonest to come here and pretend to be
alcoholic. And I'm an honest person.

MARY   I think you're a con artist.

BOB   No need to get hostile, now, just because *you* can't
drink . . .

LEADER   I'm afraid I have to agree with Mary, Bob. Most of
you know I'm a recovering alcoholic myself, and I know the
games we play with ourselves to prove we can drink. I've
even played that particular game of yours once or twice.
And then after a week or two of "social drinking," I'd go off
on another bender. The truth was I was full of crap. I was
in denial.

BOB   I agree with you that an alcoholic who drinks is just
fooling himself. But I don't think I'm an alcoholic. So that
doesn't apply to me.

MARY   Phooey. You told me you had blackouts. You said you
used to drink a bottle of vodka every couple of days. What
do you think that means? You're an alcoholic. You're just
denying it.

LEADER   And didn't you say you'd been in detox once?

BOB   That was for bad stomach. The doctor never said
definitely that I was alcoholic, and I don't appreciate
getting all this . . .

MARY   I cannot stand all this bickering. I come to group to
get away from this, this fighting and arguing. I cannot
tolerate this.

LEADER   Mary, you began the group saying this was a
wonderful experience.

MARY   Well, *usually* it is, but not today. I was happy when I
got here, and now I'm miserable. That's not the way group
is supposed to work. I'm supposed to feel *better*, not worse.

LOUISE   (for the first time) I have a comment.

LEADER   Go ahead, Louise.

LOUISE   It seems to me that Bob is just trying to see if we'll get all upset because he had a couple of drinks. It's like little kid seeing if you'll get mad at him for breaking a rule. He just wants to know if we really mean it.

BOB   Why would I care what you all think about my drinking?

LOUISE   I think you care more than you admit. You're a very insecure person, underneath that tough shell, I think.

BOB   Jesus Christ.

MARY   Well, why don't you try listening for a change, Bob. You might *learn* something.

LOUISE   You see, I think Bob really wants us all to notice him, and having a drink is a sure way to get attention. He knows we'll all be disturbed. If we ignore it, I think Bob will just give up and stop drinking. It's not really the liquor he wants. It's the attention.

LEADER   What do you think of that, Bob?

BOB   I think it's a pile of horseshit.

LOUISE   And using profanity is another way of covering up your feelings.

TED   Not necessarily. I mean he doesn't have to be covering anything up. He could just like swearing. I mean, I hear people swear all the time, and I don't think you could say *they're* covering anything up.

MARY   You're as bad as Bob.

LEADER   I don't think fighting will solve anything.

TED   Especially if you're fighting with Mary. Her husband's been doing that for years, and it never got him anywhere.

LOUISE   You're an intellectual bully. You can't face your own emotions, so you try to make sure other people can't face theirs either.

LEADER   How about some of the other members of the group? I notice we only have three people contributing. Ethel, what about you?

ETHEL   Well . . . I hate profanity. It's disgusting. That's why these AA meetings bother me so much. People use words that I don't feel I have to listen to.

LEADER   Don't you think they're just being honest?

ETHEL   If that's honesty, I don't need it.

LEADER   And you, Jim? What's your reaction to what
Louise said about Bob covering up his emotions and
drinking to get attention from the group? Do you think
that's true?

JIM   I think it all depends on how you define "emotions." If
you mean your personal feelings, then yes. But if you mean
something else, then no. At least that's my opinion. It's a
question of meaning.

LEADER   Bob, where are you going?

BOB   To get some coffee. Anybody else want some?

MARY   Yes, please.

BOB   Sugar and cream?

MARY   Yes please. Two packets.

LEADER   I think that's a good way of distracting us from
the issue at hand.

TED   Not necessarily. They *could* just want a cup of coffee.

LOUISE   I think Bob and Ted are afraid of themselves.

MARY   You tell them, honey.

LOUISE   I think Bob and Ted both have low self-esteem.

MARY   Well, I don't know if it's so *low*. They seem to think
pretty highly of themselves.

LOUISE   They're overcompensating.

MARY   You know, I was sure we were finally getting some-
place in this group. But now it seems like we've gone
backwards. We've been coming here for six weeks, and it's
been nothing but a struggle. One thing after another. I'm
so *tired*.

LEADER   Are you talking about the group or about yourself,
Mary?

MARY   I don't know anymore. It seems like no one is willing
to set aside their negative feelings and work together to
grow. Isn't that what we're all here for? I mean, if we don't
have each other, what have we got?

BOB   That's fine with me. I'm sorry I ever brought up the
thing about the two drinks. If I'd kept my mouth shut,
you'd have never known. We'd have had a nice group.

TED   No, you're supposed to be honest. But I don't think we need to jump on you for telling us the truth. I mean, you have a right to your own life.

BOB   Louise, I want to apologize. I didn't mean to lose my temper with you. But when you talk that psychology stuff, you sound just like my ex-wife. She'd never leave me alone. Always trying to shrink my head. But don't take it personally.

LOUISE   That's OK. I understand, Bob. The truth hurts us all, I guess.

TED   If it is the truth. I don't think we know for sure.

MARY   Bob, I'm sorry I got mad too. I really do like you, I really do. It's just you can be so frustrating. I want to bop you on the head sometimes. But if I didn't care about you, I wouldn't feel that way, would I? It's a sign of caring, really.

BOB   I know that, Mary.

LEADER   What about the drinking, Bob? Are you going to continue your experiments? Are you going to stay with the group?

BOB   Well, I had decided to drop out, you all heard me say that. But now, I don't know. I still don't believe I'm an alcoholic, and I don't think any of you could prove to me that I was. But I see that the group has helped me. Maybe I'll stay for a while. See if I don't continue to improve. I feel I get something out of these sessions, even if I don't strictly belong. I know I don't show it all the time, but I like you people.

ETHEL   Now why can't you be like that all the time? You can be a very nice person.

BOB   I know, Ethel. It's my cursed Irish temper, I suppose.

LOUISE   You ought to work on that in the group. It's a sign of low self-esteem.

TED   You know, I think I've really gotten something out of this group.

MARY   Oh, I definitely have. I love these groups.

TED   I think Bob has really made a breakthrough tonight.

LOUISE   You may be right. He's beginning to lower his defenses. We are starting to see the real Bob.

BOB   Well, I can be a handful, I know. I thank all of you for putting up with me.

LEADER   I feel positive about this, too. I don't think Bob will ever be able to drink safely for any length of time, but I respect his willingness to hold his ideas up for discussion. That takes courage.

TED   I don't know if I could do it.

LEADER   Perhaps you will, Ted, in the next session.

TED   Well, to be honest, I have had a couple of little episodes of drinking myself in the last month. I didn't tell the group because I felt you'd all jump on me. But now I see that it's OK to admit your flaws.

LOUISE   You can be honest with us, Ted.

MARY   Oh, definitely.

BOB   That's what I like about this group. Things may not always be perfect, but we keep trying.

LOUISE   We're sometimes discouraged, but we're never defeated, are we?

MARY   Absolutely not.

LEADER   Till next week, group.

MARY   Keep coming back. And I love you all!

Bonding: _____

_____

Climate: _____

_____

Values: _____

_____

Status and traditions: _____

_____

_____

Structure: _____

_____

Mentality: _____

_____

Dominant mode: _____

_____

Other modes during session: _____

_____

_____

Discussion

Notice how, almost as soon as the group begins, Mary makes a strong attempt to set up an alliance with the leader. This is usually a sign that there has already been some type of split within the group, and Mary is making sure she is on the "right" side of whatever conflict emerges.

Curiously, the leader himself abandons the task, in favor of his own agenda concerning Ted's marital problems. This sets the stage for an "anything-is-relevant" discussion and further fragmentation of the group. Finally, Bob confronts the members with a legitimate problem: He has decided to drop out in favor of another stab at "controlled drinking."

Of course, the group is stuck in the hopeful expectation mode and can't handle a real crisis.

- *Bonding:* Negative, around the idea that everyone in the group is doing well, despite evidence to the contrary. The leader is an active participant in this bonding. A group-wide state of denial develops.
- *Climate:* Like most such groups, this one adopts a posture of

superficial high morale, for which Mary serves as cheerleader. Behind this is a background of passivity and discouragement. No one can figure out how to face the group's difficulties.

- *Values:* Strikingly, this group manages to *devalue* abstinence from alcohol. It's as though they have all forgotten that they are in an alcoholism treatment group.

    Secondly, the group clearly substitutes continued attendance for quality of interaction. As long as Bob keeps coming to the group, everyone will keep fingers crossed that he'll somehow manage presumably on his own to get sober.

    The group also values form over content: Ethel objects to cussing; Jim wants a "definition" of emotion; Ted disputes any inference that doesn't have supporting documentation. Personal preferences have become more important than successful treatment of the disease.

- *Status and traditions:* The leader is clearly allied with the active members. The group seem to have a tradition: Attendance and complimentary remarks about the group are an acceptable substitute for change.

- *Mentality:* "Hang in there, everybody. Things will get better."

- *Culture:* There will have to be a struggle between anyone who desires to change and the dominant resistance of this group. This has, in fact, ceased being an alcoholism treatment group. It is now an alcoholism *discussion* group. Anyone who wants to change will probably have to drop out.

Alternative Interventions

Once the leader allows his own curiosity about Ted to drag the group away from the task, the group is given the message that the task (and the goals of treatment) was never that important in the first place. Accordingly, when the group is confronted by Bob's relapse, it is already so far off-task that members can do little except poke feebly at Bob's defense mechanisms. There's no precedent for saying, "Bob, you're out of line . . . listening to your justifications for continued drinking is *not* the purpose of this group."

The leader should have placed very definite value on *abstinence*. That way, Bob's behavior would have immediately been identified by the group as a *relapse*, and therefore inconsistent with the goals of treatment. Instead, the group members continued to treat Bob's participation as a "positive" experience. Their challenges were superficial. As long as he seemed to participate and was willing to listen to the opinions of other members, he could continue attending the group *even as he lost control over his drinking*.

This group is in fact engaged in *enabling behavior*, helping the alcoholic to avoid recognition of the fact of his own relapse. As such, it probably does more harm than good for the suffering alcoholic.

GROUP PROCESS EXERCISE #3: AFTERCARE GROUP A

Most contemporary programs offer some form of aftercare. This is designed to ease the transition into a sober, usually AA-oriented lifestyle, and to provide ongoing support during the initial year of recovery.

In this group there are nine members, five males and four females, all of whom have been members for at least one month. There are two leaders. The group meets once weekly.

LEADER #1   Does anyone have a problem they'd like to put before the group?

(silence)

MARK   Isn't anybody going to say anything?

HELEN   What is there to say? I don't have a problem.

MARK   Then why are you in this group?

HELEN   Because the counselors made me go, like everybody else.

LEADER #2   I thought this group was voluntary.

MARK   It is.

HELEN   No, it's not. If you say you won't go, they give you a lot of grief until you give in.

LEADER #2   What do you mean by grief?

HELEN   They told me if I didn't go to aftercare I'd get
   drunk.
MARK   So what? Isn't that true?
HELEN   I don't happen to think so, no.
LEADER #2   Why do you think the counselors believed you'd
   relapse if you didn't go to aftercare? Did you ask them?
HELEN   Sure I asked. They said my history showed I'd get
   drunk if I didn't follow their directions.
LEADER #2   How so? Had you relapsed before?
HELEN   Twice.
LEADER #2   Both times after going through treatment
   programs?
HELEN   Yes. Once in the 1970s, and once last year.
LEADER #1   I think that constitutes a problem. That's the
   kind of thing we can work on in this group.
HELEN   What for? That's ancient history.
MARK   They mean work on preventing the *next* relapse.
HELEN   Here you go again. I don't see why everybody
   expects me to get drunk again. I know what I did wrong,
   and I changed it.
LEADER #2   And what was it you changed?
HELEN   My problem was that I went to AA for a while, but
   then I stopped going.
LEADER #2   How long would you go before you stopped?
HELEN   Maybe six or eight weeks.
LEADER #2   Then you'd get drunk again.
HELEN   I wouldn't get drunk. I'd start drinking a little
   wine. I wouldn't get drunk until later.
LEADER #1   So you left the program last year, and stayed
   sober how long?
HELEN   A couple of months.
LEADER #1   Then you started drinking wine. Did you stick
   to wine?
HELEN   No, I switched to vodka.
LEADER #1   And then what happened?
HELEN   Well, I drank vodka for about three months without
   getting in trouble – bad trouble – but then my husband got
   mad because I was forgetting conversations and not

making dinner again, and he said if I didn't come in the hospital he'd divorce me.

MARK   I've heard that myself.

LEADER #1   Have any of the rest of you in the group gotten warnings like that from your loved ones?

(silence for five or ten seconds. Members look at each other.)

MARK   I imagine everyone has.

HELEN   You don't know that. Let them speak for themselves.

LEADER #2   Was that the first time you got such a threat from your husband?

HELEN   No. The first time, my whole family got together and confronted me. That was when I went into the first treatment program.

LEADER #1   How did you feel about that?

HELEN   I've never forgiven them. Pious bastards. Holier than thou.

LEADER #1   So you've never forgiven them. You have a resentment.

HELEN   I don't have a resentment. I *did* have one. Now I just don't care.

MARK   You are really full of it, Helen.

HELEN   Stuff it, Mark.

(Both smile.)

LEADER #2   So how about since you left this program, Helen? Have you been going to AA regularly?

HELEN   Yes, I have.

MARK   I haven't seen you.

HELEN   Do you go to every meeting in the area?

MARK   No, but I live two blocks from you, and I go to the meetings you would go to, if you went.

HELEN   I've been to at least two meetings a week.

MARK   Which week?

HELEN   Look . . .

LEADER #1   Is that what you agreed to on your aftercare plan, Helen? Two meetings a week?

HELEN   No.

LEADER #1   How many did you agree to?

HELEN   Six a week.

LEADER #2   So even if you've gone to two a week, you've still broken your agreement. And you're only six weeks out of the program.

HELEN   Look, I don't have to put up with this. Why don't you ask any of these other people? How do you know *they're* going to AA?

LEADER #2   It's you we're talking to, Helen. It's your program that seems weak. In fact, it looks like you're doing exactly the same thing you did after the *last* program.

MARK   Which I've been telling you all along.

HELEN   I am *not* doing the same thing. This is *different*. The circumstances are completely changed.

LEADER #2   In what way? You went through a program because your husband threatened to leave you. You agreed to attend six AA meetings a week for the first months afterwards. You immediately cut back to two a week, and I imagine you'll cut those out within the next month. How is that different from what you did before?

HELEN   Before, I had been drinking for a long time. This time, I was only drinking a few months, and I wasn't nearly as sick.

LEADER #2   How sick do you have to be, Helen, before you get rid of this denial?

MARK   No kidding.

LEADER #1   Helen, do you believe you have a progressive, fatal disease?

HELEN   What do you mean? I said I was an alcoholic.

LEADER #1   Saying you're an alcoholic is one thing. Believing you have a fatal disease is another. Do you believe that if you continue drinking, you will die of alcoholism?

HELEN   I know that.

LEADER #2   Then how do you justify dropping out of AA, which you know is the only effective treatment?

HELEN   I don't justify it. I know I have to go.

LEADER #1   Then why don't you?

HELEN   Because it is so damned *boring*. Those stories make me want to get drunk. I don't want to hear about other people's problems. I have plenty of my own. I am sick to death of hearing about alcohol, alcohol, alcohol. I feel like everybody wants you to become a *fanatic*. When do you get time for yourself? I have other needs, you know. Life can't be all AA and alcoholism, you know.

LEADER #2   When you drink, do you drink every day?

HELEN   Of course. You know that.

LEADER #2   And do you drink all evening long?

MARK   And half the afternoon, I'll bet.

HELEN   I don't see your point.

LEADER #1   The point is that if you devote as much time to staying sober as you do to drinking, you'd probably get sober easily.

LEADER #2   But instead, you try to get sober by going to a couple of meetings a week. That's not a one to one exchange.

HELEN   OK, I understand. You're right.

LEADER #2   I think you're just going along to get us off your case.

HELEN   No. I see you *are* right. This is how I got into trouble last time. I started to resent the meetings. I thought it was unfair that I had to go, while my husband got to stay home and watch TV.

LEADER #2   Do you really think life is fair? Does his behavior change what you have to do to get sober and stay sober?

HELEN   No. It's my responsibility. And I'm letting it go again.

LEADER #2   So what will you do to *change* that pattern?

HELEN   I'll make more meetings.

LEADER #1   How will you do that? And how will you deal with your resentments about having to go?

MARK   You can go with me. We can criticize the speakers together. As long as we're sober, we can say whatever we want.

HELEN   (laughs) I guess that would be more fun. And we do get along pretty well, even though you'd never know it.

LEADER #1   We're running short of time. Did any of the

other members – there are a few of you who have been quiet
tonight – have anything to add?
(Silence. Members look at one another, saying nothing.)
LEADER #1   All right. We'll meet again Tuesday. And you
get to some meetings before then, OK?
HELEN   All right.

Bonding: _____

_____

Climate: _____

_____

Values: _____

_____

_____

Status and traditions: _____

_____

_____

Structure: _____

_____

Mentality: _____

_____

Dominant mode: _____

_____

Other modes during session: _____

_____

_____

Discussion

This is a perfect example of a group that isn't a group. It never leaves the helpless mode, and no attempt is made by the designated leaders to generate or make use of group process. In fact, this is individual counseling with an audience.

- *Bonding:* Negative, around the idea that all wisdom and insight come from the designated Leaders.
- *Climate:* The group provides "designated patients" on whom the leaders can demonstrate their therapy skills, and an appreciative audience (Mark) for their activities.
- *Values:* All roles are assigned by the leaders, who might decide in another session that Mark or another member is "it" for that week. Helen, subject of attention in the session recorded here, might take over Mark's role as Greek chorus for the leaders.
- *Status:* Entirely leader-oriented.
- *Traditions:* None. If the designated leadership changed, this group would have to transmogrify its orientation to fit the new leaders.
- *Structure:* This group is structured to allow the leaders to confront selected patients at will, without challenge.
- *Mentality:* The group does not think. It reacts to direction.
- *Culture:* A chronic conflict between the group's dependent stance (vis-à-vis the leader) and any member who sought to express autonomy or independence.

Alternative Interventions

This group is so dependent – and the leaders have so firmly established their role as all-knowing therapists – that the mem-

bers will no doubt feel quite betrayed if the leaders stop directing and controlling discussion. Nevertheless, that's exactly
what must happen for this to become a work group. So we
would suggest that the leaders simply stop doing what they're
doing, inform the members of their responsibility for the group
and for their own recovery, and let the chips fall where they
may. Of course, there may be a few dropouts, but that's to be
expected. Because both Mark and Helen have the potential to
be something more than actors in the therapist's little drama,
the overall prognosis for the group is better than we might
expect, provided the designated leaders get out of the way.

GROUP PROCESS EXERCISE #4:
AFTERCARE GROUP B

This group meets once weekly, with the stated purpose of
assisting members in making the transition into a sober lifestyle. All members have been in aftercare at least one month.
There are six members present, as well as two designated leaders.

LEADER #1   The topic for today is how communicating with
other people can help you avoid relapse. That might include
communications at home, at AA, at work, and so on.
(silence for several minutes)
TOBY   I think this may be the longest silence we've had.
This is even longer than the silence when the topic was sex
and the alcoholic.
SUSIE   Hey, let's not get off into alcohol again, OK? I don't
even drink, and I always have to listen to that talk about
booze. Let's discuss something else.
TOD   Oops, we forgot. We have a junkie in the group.
SUSIE   (makes a gesture and smiles) Climb this, lushbrain.
TOD   (grabs heart) Ooh, I love it when you talk dirty.
TOBY   Let's get on with it, guys. We're just wasting time.
What about some of the rest of you? We do all the talking
in these groups. How do *you* communicate with people?

FRANK   (slowly) I'm not exactly sure what you mean by
"communicate."

SUSIE   Talk. Relate. You know.

FRANK   I'm still not exactly sure I understand . . .

TOD   Is that it, or would you just rather not talk, and this is
how you avoid offering an opinion?

FRANK   You don't have to be rude.

TOD   I'm not trying to be. But you're always worrying about
the exact meaning of words, and that's pretty irrelevant. I
bet you have problems communicating with people.

FRANK   Listen, young man, I was a journalist for 30 years.
You can't be a journalist and not know how to communicate.

JEAN   My ex-husband was a journalist, and he couldn't
communicate at all, unless you let him write you an editorial with footnotes. We never talked about *anything*.

SUSIE   How long were you married?

JEAN   Eleven years.

SUSIE   Sounds like a wonderful marriage.

JEAN   It was better than my second one. He was a drunk.

TOD   Two of you in the same household, huh?

JEAN   (angry) I am *not* a drunk. I wasn't a drunk *then*. I
have a drinking problem which I have under control.

FRANK   You don't mean you're still drinking, do you?

JEAN   (hesitates) I don't . . . oh, I don't know why I should
hide it. I have an occasional glass of wine after dinner.
Nothing more. No vodka, if that's what you think.

FRANK   I don't think any drinking at all is wise. I know how
much trouble you've had in the past.

JEAN   That's *your* opinion.

TOD   Looks like denial time again, folks. We've discovered a
nonalcoholic in this group.

BILL   I wish you wouldn't make fun of everyone.

TOD   Hitting close to home, huh?

BILL   No, you're not. But you jump on everybody who talks.

FRANK   He's right in this case, though. Jean is drinking

again, and we ought to make every attempt to convince her
to stop.

SUSIE   Why bother? I don't think she wants to stop.

TOBY   Nobody ever does. That's why we end up in treatment
programs. We don't want to stop until we're in trouble
again.

JEAN   I'm not in any trouble.

FRANK   Not yet, Jean, but you will be.

JIM   I have to agree, Jean. I've done this myself. You get
away with it for a while, then it gets out of control?

TOBY   How did you start?

JEAN   What do you mean? I just decided, is all. I'm an
adult.

TOD   You'd never know it.

JEAN   (angry) How dare you! What right do you have to sit
in judgment! You're no better than the rest of us!

TOD   That's true. But I *am* sober.

JEAN   Don't criticize me! I happen to think you're a homo-
sexual! But you don't see me throwing that in your face!

TOD   Then what is this I'm wiping off right now? Custard
pie?

FRANK   I don't think Tod's sexuality is our concern, Jean.
This is a group for alcoholics. When you tell such a group
you are drinking, you should expect a strong reaction.

SUSIE   Jean, does your husband know you've started again?

JEAN   I don't know.

SUSIE   What do you think he'll do when he finds out?

JEAN   I have no idea.

SUSIE   Didn't he say he'd divorce you? Didn't he say he'd
move out?

JEAN   He might have. I don't remember.

SUSIE   This is your third husband, Jean. Do you want to
lose him?

JEAN   (tearful) Of course not.

TOBY   Then why are you risking everything just to be able
to drink a glass of wine with dinner?

JEAN   I don't know. I do it, and it makes sense at the time, but then I regret it, and I swear I won't have any more. But a few days later, I have another one.

BILL   Can you stop after one?

JEAN   Usually... but last week I really blew it. I got stinking drunk... finished a bottle in about an hour. Thank God my husband was out of town. The next day, I felt awful.

BILL   Did you call your sponsor? Ask for help?

JEAN   My sponsor is out of town.

SUSIE   Why don't you get another one, like a backup? I have three. One couldn't handle me. I'm too weird.

TOD   No shit.

TOBY   Kill the humor, Tod. Jean, do you have a home group?

JEAN   Yes, St. Patrick's. I like it.

TOBY   Why don't you ask somebody there to be your second sponsor?

JEAN   All right. I know some people.

SUSIE   That should help.

JEAN   I feel better. Thank you.

FRANK   I don't think we've solved this problem.

BILL   What do you mean?

FRANK   I don't think Jean can quit drinking on her own. I think she needs to go back in the program.

JEAN   (wails) Nooooo...

BILL   Now see what you've done.

FRANK   Stop rescuing her, Bill. She's just told you she can't stop. What makes you think getting another sponsor is the way to stop now?

SUSIE   True. My sponsor—one of them—told me AA can help you *stay* stopped, but sometimes you have to go into the program to *get* stopped.

JEAN   I *can't*. My husband will divorce me.

SUSIE   I think he'll divorce you if you *don't* get help. Do you really think you can hide it from him for long?

JEAN   Oh my God, I can't lose him, I just can't...

FRANK   I don't think you will if you get help and tell him the truth.

BILL   I think we're way out of our league here. We're not
experts. I think the leaders ought to make this decision.

LEADER #1   I think Jean has to make it.

BILL   But what are you guys here for if not to tell us how to
stay sober?

FRANK   This is a group, Bill. We're supposed to tell each
other how to stay sober.

BILL   *I'm* no expert . . .

TOBY   You don't need an expert, Bill. You know what Jean
ought to do. So does everybody in this group.

TOD   Even me. I think you ought to go into the program,
Jean.

JEAN   You! Who asked you! You're a . . .

TOD   I know, I'm a faggot. I'm also an alcoholic. If you can't
relate to one, you can relate to the other.

TOBY   Tod isn't your problem, Jean. Your problem is: Are
you going to admit you've blown it and get back into the
program? Or are you going to pretend for a while longer
and back yourself into a corner where your husband gets
mad and dumps you?

JEAN   You have such a sensitive way of putting it.

FRANK   It's the truth.

SUSIE   Is this how you lost the other marriages, Jean? You
wouldn't admit there was anything wrong? You were so
afraid of blowing your marriage that you blew your marriage?

TOD   Is that sentence in English?

SUSIE   You know what I mean.

BILL   And we were supposed to discuss communication.
Seems to me Jean needs to communicate with her husband.

TOBY   True. But first she needs to quit drinking.

FRANK   That has to come first.

JEAN   Why? I'm not out of control yet.

FRANK   Yes, you are. You're not *totally* out of control, but
you are out of control.

TOD   There's another one of those sentences.

SUSIE   What's that defense mechanism, the one that Tod
always uses?

TOBY   Intellectualization.
SUSIE   That's it. There you go, Tod. The next time you
   get ready to say something, just think, "I'm getting
   ready to intellectualize again." And try saying something
   else.
TOD   Touché.
FRANK   What about it, Jean? What are you going to do?
JEAN   I'm going to think about it.
SUSIE   Haven't you been thinking about it for the last few
   weeks? Why don't you just decide?
JEAN   I have to take it up with my husband first.
SUSIE   Why? Don't you think he'll be more receptive if he
   knows you voluntarily sought some help, instead of waiting
   for him to force you?
JEAN   I suppose that's true.
SUSIE   So decide. Now.
JEAN   I can't. I have to think about it. I'm not the kind of
   person who does things on impulse.
BILL   You *drink* on impulse.
JEAN   That's different.
FRANK   Only in your eyes, Jean. You need to take action,
   now.
JEAN   Here's what I'll do. I'll think about it, and when my
   husband gets back, he and I may sit down and discuss it.
   Then I'll let you all know my decision. All right?
FRANK   How long before we hear the result?
JEAN   Well, he won't be back for two weeks . . . and then it
   will be another week before we have a chance to talk. . . . I'll
   let you know within a month.
SUSIE   You plan to put this off for a month? Do you really
   think you can keep it together?
JEAN   Yes.
BILL   Now even I have to object to *that*. . . . It's asking too
   much of yourself, Jean. You're an alcoholic.
JEAN   Nevertheless, that's my decision. I'll just have to ask
   you all to be patient.
SUSIE   What will you do for treatment during that month,
   Jean?

JEAN   What do you mean?

LEADER #2   We have a boundary that no one who relapses can remain in aftercare unless they enter the program again.

JEAN   No! If my husband finds out I'm not in aftercare, he'll know I got kicked out! He'll find out about my slip! Listen, I'll stop on my own. I haven't had anything in almost a week. But I have to stay in the group.

SUSIE   You know they won't change the boundary. It's enter the program or be terminated from the group.

JEAN   This is so unfair! I didn't have to tell you about the drinking! You're taking my freedom away!

FRANK   They're just giving you a clear choice, Jean. They're not trying to punish you.

JEAN   (defeated) All right. I'll go in next week, after the Garden Show.

SUSIE   I think they mean you have to go in now, Jean. Or get kicked out of Aftercare.

FRANK   I'm sure of it, Jean. They're not going to make a deal.

TOBY   Well, we're out of time, I guess. I have to be going anyway. Do you want me to give you a ride to the program, Jean? I'm going over tomorrow morning.

JEAN   I guess I have to.

TOBY   I'll see you at 9.

SUSIE   We'll come by and visit. You'll be back in the group in no time.

FRANK   She's right, Jean.

LEADER   That's all our time for this week.

Bonding: _____

_____

Climate: _____

_____

Values: _____

_____

_____

Status and traditions: _____

_____

_____

Structure: _____

_____

Mentality: _____

_____

Dominant mode: _____

_____

Other modes during session: _____

_____

_____

Discussion

This group starts with the usual signs of helplessness, flirts with hostility, and then, quite surprisingly, turns into an excellent example of a work group.

• *Bonding:* The group bonds positively around a task, but not the one set forth at the beginning by the designated leader. Clearly, "communication" is not really an important issue for this group. A much more crucial concern – relapse by a member – is the focus of their bonding.

- *Climate:* Morale is high, once the group finds its focus. In addition, the group refuses to accept an unworkable compromise – a promise by Jean to quit drinking on her own – and thus reaffirms its commitment to the goals of treatment, rather than to easy solutions.
- *Values:* When various members of the group try to abdicate responsibility, other members block the attempt. For example, when Bill tries to turn responsibility for a decision over to the "experts," Frank and Toby prevent it. The group obviously places high value on autonomous decision-making.

   Also, there is evident value placed on abstinence. No one in the group ever questions that Jean has relapsed or that this is counterproductive to treatment. Clearly, this group takes itself seriously and its members' recovery is preeminent in its thinking.
- *Status:* Roles within the group are extremely flexible, which is characteristic of the work mode. Frank, seemingly resistant early in the group, is a leader by its end. The designated leader really figures little in the group's process until its conclusion.
- *Traditions, structure:* These follow naturally from the work mode. If the work is sustained and becomes the dominant form of interaction within the group, then we may assume that structure will flow from the traditions established by the membership. This is the first group we've studied that has rules about boundaries; Jean is told clearly that she cannot remain in the aftercare group while drinking and making up her mind about entering a program. The boundary doesn't change.
- *Mentality:* Only sobriety – and stable sobriety, at that – is acceptable.
- *Culture:* The group's goals are to be maintained despite resistance or challenge by individual members.

Alternative Interventions

Really, none are necessary. The leaders stepped in only to do what the group itself could not: establish and maintain the boundary on participation after a relapse. They wisely didn't see Jean's crisis as a call for them to take over the discussion.

It isn't difficult to see that, if two new leaders showed up at the next session, this group would be capable of continuing to work without interruption.

GROUP PROCESS EXERCISE #5:
FIRST STEP GROUP

Another popular group is the first step group, where members examine their own histories for signs of powerlessness and inability to manage alcohol.

In this session, there are five members and the leader. All members have been patients less than two weeks. It takes place in an inpatient setting.

LEADER   I guess we can go ahead and start now. Jim, are you all settled yet? Is anybody missing? Ralph? Marion, would you go ask one of the staff members to find Ralph and send him in here?

OK. Well, the purpose of this group is to help those of you who are new in the program take your first step. I suppose I ought to read the step out loud for those of you who aren't familiar with it: "We admitted we were powerless over alcohol – that our lives had become unmanageable."

So when you take your first step, you have to look honestly at your drinking and ask yourself the question: Am I powerless over alcohol? And then you have to look honestly at your life in general and ask a second question: Has my life become unmanageable?

Marion, what about you? Can you say you have become powerless over alcohol?

MARION   Yes, I very honestly can say that I am powerless
over alcohol.

DAVID   I can't.

LEADER   Why not?

DAVID   Because I don't really believe that is true.

LEADER   I know that. What I'm asking is what makes you
believe it *isn't* true?

DAVID   I don't have to prove to you I'm innocent. That's not
the way the American legal system works. You have to
prove I'm *guilty*.

LEADER   That's an unusual way to view a disease – as an
issue of guilt or innocence.

DAVID   I don't believe it's a disease.

LEADER   What do you think alcoholism is?

DAVID   It's a way of coping with stress.

LEADER   Stress? Give us an example.

DAVID   Well . . . like if you were in a bad marriage or something, and your wife drove you crazy, you might drink to
get back at her.

LEADER   Have you ever done that?

DAVID   Wait a minute . . . you're twisting my words. You
asked me for an example. I didn't say it had anything to do
with me.

LEADER   Are you married?

DAVID   I refuse to answer that.

LEADER   David, you're not in court. Nothing you say is
being recorded. We presume you're here because you have
some sort of problem with alcohol. This group is a place for
you to begin identifying and treating that problem.

DAVID   All right, all right . . . don't get mad at me.

LEADER   I'm not angry. But you're going to have to open up
a bit to get anything out of being here.

DAVID   Give me another day or two, will you? I just don't
feel like I'm ready yet. It's just too traumatic. I'll jump in
occasionally, but I'd rather not be on the hot seat yet, if
that's OK with you.

LEADER   Sure. We'll get back to you tomorrow.

MARION   I think you're letting him off pretty easy.

LEADER   Didn't we lay off you a couple of days when you first got here?

MARION   No. You jumped on me the minute I arrived.

LEADER   It wasn't that rough, Marion.

MARION   I sure felt bad. Maybe it wasn't that rough on *you*.

LEADER   That surprises me, Marion, to hear that from you. You always seem so calm.

MARION   Maybe on the outside. But I get hurt like anyone else.

LEADER   When we started today, I asked you if you were powerless over alcohol. You said you were. Did you really mean it or were you just saying that to placate me?

MARION   I really meant it, but I didn't want you on my back, either.

LEADER   Do you really perceive discussing the fact that you're an alcoholic as being on your back?

MARION   Sometimes. But I understand it's necessary. Except it bothers me when I see you be so easy on David. Because he's just as alcoholic as the rest of us, and I don't see why he gets special treatment.

DAVID   I don't think I'm getting special treatment.

LEADER   David will have to take the first step, like everyone else. The only question is when.

DAVID   I want to take it now.

LEADER   You do?

DAVID   Well, if people are going to get all *upset* about it, I'll go ahead and do it. I mean, I didn't know it was going to cause such a *fuss*.

MARION   I am *not* upset.

LEADER   All right, David. Describe to us how you are powerless over alcohol.

DAVID   Sometimes when I drink I have trouble stopping.

LEADER   All the time?

DAVID   No, just once in a while.

LEADER   How often? Once a week?

DAVID   Oh no . . . more like once a month, or once every five or six weeks.

LEADER   Describe an episode where you can't quit drinking.

DAVID   Oh I can quit, but it takes a little effort.

MARION   It sounds to me like you don't think you belong here.

DAVID   What do you mean?

MARION   If *I* only had a problem every six weeks, I wouldn't check into the hospital.

DAVID   Well, that's you.

JIM   (speaking for the first time) That's anybody. I mean, no way I'd be here if I had your problem. You sound like a social drinker or something. Why are you here?

DAVID   My wife was complaining, and I'm a good husband, and I want her to be happy.

MARION   So you came here for her sake.

DAVID   Are you attacking me?

LEADER   No. I think the group is just curious as to what made your wife think you had a problem with alcohol.

DAVID   She's a teetotaler. She doesn't drink at all. She became born again about four years ago.

JIM   So what does that have to do with you?

DAVID   It doesn't have anything to do with me. He asked, so I told him.

MARION   Does your wife have anything to do with why you drink?

DAVID   Absolutely nothing.

LEADER   Why do you drink, David?

DAVID   To relax.

LEADER   Relax from what? What makes you tense?

DAVID   People.

LEADER   At work? At home?

DAVID   Just people.

MARION   Well, if people make you tense, you'll probably end up drunk for the rest of your life, because there are a lot of people in the world.

JIM   Sounds like an excuse to me.

DAVID   What do you mean?

LEADER   I think Jim feels that you're not being altogether honest about which people make you tense. For example, your relationship with your wife.

MARION   That would be a place to start. What happened
with your wife to cause you to come here?

DAVID   We had a fight, but it wasn't about drinking.

LEADER   What was it about?

DAVID   I don't want to say.

JIM   Then I think you'd *better* say. No use hiding it. We all
have the same problem, you know.

DAVID   I don't have the same problem. I am an individual.
None of us are exactly the same. We are all unique.

LEADER   OK, David, settle down a bit. Nobody is questioning your uniqueness. But Jim is right: You ought to share
what's wrong with this group.

DAVID   I spent too much money when I was drunk one
weekend.

JIM   You mean you bought drinks for everybody in the bar.

DAVID   Perhaps.

MARION   "Perhaps"? What do you mean, "perhaps"?

DAVID   Just exactly what I said. Perhaps. I may have spent
the money buying drinks for everyone in a bar. I've done
that before. And my wife got mad about it.

JIM   Were you in town here when you did it?

DAVID   What do you mean?

JIM   Where was the bar that you spent all this money in?

DAVID   How do you know I spent it in a bar? I didn't say
that's what happened. I happen to be very responsible with
my money. I am an accountant, for God's sake. Don't go
spreading it around that I throw money away in bars. Are
you trying to ruin my career?

MARION   Jesus, you're touchy. You implied you spent it in a
bar. Then you say you didn't say you spent it in a bar.
Which is it?

DAVID   That's my affair.

JIM   Wait a minute. I am beginning to get the picture.
Dave, you may have spent the money in a bar, or maybe
you didn't, right?

DAVID   It's perfectly clear to me.

JIM   Are you not exactly *sure* what you did with the money?

DAVID   Not completely.

JIM   You don't remember?

DAVID   I remember a lot, very clearly. There are some parts
I don't remember, and what I did with the money is one of
them.

LEADER   David, how much money are we talking about?

DAVID   I don't think ethically I can reveal that.

LEADER   Nothing leaves this room, David. No one here
knows your last name. I'm bound by laws of confidentiality.
You can tell the truth.

DAVID $35,000.

MARION   You spent $35,000?

DAVID   I don't know that I *spent* it. I might have *lost* it. I
might have been *robbed*.

LEADER   Start at the beginning, David.

DAVID   I had a fight with my wife. I had been drinking for
five or six days. Before that I had been sober for a whole
month. I took the money out of our private account and
out of my company account. I know how to do that. I'm an
accountant. I'm self-employed, so I didn't steal any money.
I do not know where the money went.

JIM   Do you remember taking it out of the bank?

DAVID   Yes. I was really mad, madder than I've ever been in
my life. I was going to move to California and start over.

MARION   Did you go to California?

DAVID   I have no idea.

JIM   How long is the gap in your memory?

DAVID   A few days.

JIM   Three? Four?

DAVID   Maybe ten.

LEADER   Was this right before you came in the hospital?

DAVID   About a week before.

LEADER   And this is why you came in?

DAVID   Yes. I also got arrested for drunk driving.

LEADER   I see. What was your BAL when you were arrested?

DAVID   I don't know.

JIM   Let me get this straight. You were sober for a month.
Then you started drinking and drank pretty much continu-

ally for five or six days. Then you got in a fight with your wife — over the drinking, right? — and you decided to take all this money out of the bank and start over in another state. Ten days later, you got arrested for a DWI, and that scared you enough you decided to stop drinking. You couldn't stop on your own, so you ended up here. You remember nothing of what you did during those ten days, including what happened to the money. Do you remember getting the DWI?

DAVID   No. They put me in the drunk tank because they said I fought the policeman who stopped me. That's the first thing I remember, waking up in the tank. My wife bailed me out, and I started drinking as soon as I got home. I was afraid I'd get in more trouble, so I checked into the program.

MARION   That's quite a story.

DAVID   I think in my own mind that I could have stopped on my own.

MARION   Then your own mind is crazy.

DAVID   Perhaps.

JIM   Crazy like an alcoholic, David. Only alcoholics behave that way.

DAVID   I know that.

JIM   You just took your first step.

LEADER   Welcome to the group.

Bonding: _____

_____

Climate: _____

_____

Values: _____

_____

Status and traditions: _____

_____

_____

Mentality: _____

_____

Structure: _____

_____

Dominant mode: _____

_____

Other modes during session: _____

_____

_____

Discussion

Here the group moves quickly into a position of mild passive hostility. The leader makes the fatal mistake of trying to remedy this through one-to-one interactions with group members that do produce insights but effectively undermine the group's evolution towards maturity and work.

It may seem that we're being too hard on this leader, because, after all, some members do benefit from their involvement in this session. But remember, we're evaluating a *group* rather than the individual participants. It's an important distinction, and one that is best illustrated with the following question: If the leader were hit by a bus before tomorrow's session, would this group know how to work in his absence? And the answer here is probably not.

- *Bonding:* Negative, around the idea that the task is unfair and perhaps even harmful to the participants. Eventually the leader gives in and begins individual counseling with various members.
- *Climate:* Initially one of suspiciousness and low morale. The mood seems to improve slightly as the session continues, probably because the leader takes the focus off the members and allows them to be an audience for his therapy session with David.
- *Values:* Like most resistant groups, this one values personal comfort over performance of the task. Members complain about how "hard" the leader is on eveyone and about how early it is to expect them to take any responsibility.
- *Status and traditions:* This group is basically leader-oriented. Jim's eventual participation is naturally modeled on the designated leader's example; he becomes a cotherapist. If the leader weren't present for the next session, Jim would probably adopt the role of primary therapist and pick somebody in the group for another one-to-one counseling session.
- *Mentality:* In the hostile mode, the group operates on the assumption that work would be an unreasonable expectation and the leader is wrong for demanding it.
- *Culture:* Conflict between the leader and the members over the issue of performing the task.

Alternative Interventions

The leader might have:

1. Had the group present the task (read step one);
2. Concentrated on involving the other members who remained silent;
3. Directed questions and comments to the group rather than directly to individual members;
4. Related the discussion to the task where appropriate.

Our guess is that the Leader became so preoccupied with helping David achieve a personal breakthrough that he used that end to justify virtually ignoring the rest of the group.

GROUP PROCESS EXERCISE #6:
MULTIPLE FAMILY GROUP

This particular group is made up of three married couples, with the husband in each couple being the alcoholic. The group is held in an inpatient treatment center, but two of the couples have been in treatment for six weeks and are returning for the group on an outpatient basis. The third couple is very new to the program and is attending the group for the first time. There are two leaders.

LEADER #1   I want to welcome two new members to our family group tonight. They are Ted and Janet. Ted is a patient in the program, and Janet is his wife. Why don't we introduce ourselves to them?

(Other members introduce themselves to the newcomers.)

Have you all had a chance to read the articles and handouts on family group? Then do you have any questions before we start?

TED   Yes. Is this what they mean on the schedule by "multiple family therapy group"?

LEADER #1   Yes.

JANET   Ted, you know that.

TED   Just checking. Things around here don't always start when they're supposed to, so I was trying to make sure this is really the 7 o'clock group. The 4 o'clock lecture started at 4:30, you know.

LEADER #1   This is the 7 p.m. group, Ted. And we start on time.

TED   No, you don't.

LEADER #1   What?

TED   It's 7:15 now. The group was to start at 7.

JANET   Ted, stop it.

LEADER   Janet, I sense some conflict between you and Ted over this issue. Is this typical of your conflicts outside the program?

TED   Not at all.

JANET   Absolutely.

LEADER #2   You seem to disagree.

JANET   Well, Ted is a perfectionist. He's always picking on the children. "You'll be late," he tells them. Drives them crazy.

TED   What does that have to do with alcoholism?

LEADER #2   Alcoholics are often perfectionists, Ted. Did you know that?

TED   I'd like to see some proof of that.

JANET   You are *living* proof of that.

BEN   It's true, Ted. When I first got here, I had a lot of problems with perfectionism. But these groups have helped me become more tolerant of others. The problem was really that I didn't like myself, so I couldn't like others.

TED   What does that have to do with alcoholism?

MARGARET   It has everything to do with it, Ted. Alcoholics drink because they are frustrated. Nine times out of ten, the thing they are most frustrated with is other people. Especially their families. So if they learn how to be less frustrated, they won't have reason to drink.

TED   How do you know that? I mean, it seems like such a sweeping generalization.

JANET   There you go again, absolutely refusing to cooperate.

TED   There *you* go again, getting angry because I ask an honest question.

LEADER #2   Are you really asking an honest question, Ted? Or are you trying to intellectualize your real feelings?

LEADER #1   You see, Ted, sometimes we all want to hide ourselves from others. We feel that if those close to us don't see our real vulnerability, we can maintain a degree of power in our relationships. We pretend we can't be hurt, which makes others think we're stronger than we really are. We can distance people, make them fear us. We become powerful. And one of the ways alcoholics control other people is through drinking.

BEN   It's true, Ted. You drink in order to have power in relationships. In order to stay sober, you're going to have to learn to become assertive rather than controlling, to get your needs met without manipulating through alcohol.

MARGARET   And at first, Ted, this will all seem strange to
you, but as time passes, you will see the truth in what we're
saying.

TED   Wait a minute. Why can't I just quit drinking?

BEN   (chuckles) If you could do that, you wouldn't be here,
Ted. You need family counseling and family therapy. You're
wife needs Alanon, and your kids need Alateen. And if
you've got any pets, you ought to send them to Aladog and
Alacat.

(Everyone laughs.)

LEADER #1   Why don't you just observe for a while, Ted,
while we examine some of the other problems that group
members have. Then things will seem clearer to you.

TED   Fair enough.

LEADER #1   Joe and Elizabeth, what about you? Last week
we talked about your approach to some problems you were
having with sex. What's happened in the interim?

ELIZABETH   I'm afraid we're not doing very well.

LEADER #1   How do you mean?

ELIZABETH   Well, we've tried to have sex every night this
week. And Joe hasn't been able to . . . well, perform.

LEADER #1   Joe?

JOE   I try, but it just doesn't work.

TED   Maybe it's left over from the drinking.

LEADER #1   I don't think so, Ted. Joe hasn't had a drink in
over a month.

TED   Oh.

LEADER #1   How about your relationship in other ways?

JOE   It's good. We have a few conflicts, but not many.

LEADER #1   Let's take a look at one of those conflicts.

ELIZABETH   We had a fight about the kids. Our son is
dating a girl we don't like.

LEADER #2   Why don't you like her?

JOE   She's not Catholic.

ELIZABETH   That's not the only thing. She hangs around
with kids who do drugs.

LEADER   And why do you argue about this? It sounds like
both of you dislike her. Where is *your* disagreement?

JOE   I think I should tell the kid to stay the hell away from that girl. Elizabeth thinks we should keep our mouths shut or we'll alienate him.

TED   How does this affect your sex life?

JOE   I don't think it does.

LEADER #2   I'd be surprised if it didn't. These are the kinds of conflicts that lead to sex problems.

TED   Janet and I fight all the time about the kids, and we have a great sex life.

JANET   It's the *only* thing we do well together, Ted. Our relationship outside of sex is terrible.

TED   That's not the point. If fighting over the kids – or over anything for that matter – makes for a bad sex life, then why don't we have a bad sex life?

LEADER #2   Don't you and Janet ever have problems with impotence?

TED   Yeah, when I'm on a bender. The rest of the time, we're OK. But after a bender, there is a two- or three-week period when my libido is down.

LEADER #1   Ted, I think you are in denial. You are attributing all your problems to alcohol, and you're not taking a look at any of your emotional problems.

TED   I thought I was here to quit drinking. I thought relating your life problems to your drinking was good, because it motivated you to quit.

LEADER #2   Ted, you don't have a drinking problem. You have a *living* problem. Alcoholic drinking is a symptom.

TED   What?

BEN   Your attitude disappoints me, Ted. You aren't making an honest effort to get help.

TED   Dammit, I *am* making an honest effort to get help. *You* are refusing to help me.

LEADER #2   We aren't refusing, Ted. But if you think we're going to let you believe you can just quit drinking without getting therapy for your life problems, you're mistaken. Quitting drinking is just the *start* of recovery. The real work lies ahead.

LEADER #1   You're going to have to get to know yourself.

TED   I *do* know myself. I'm an alcoholic.

JANET   Ted, if you keep this up, I'm walking right out of here.

TED   Then go. I came here because you told me I could get help quitting drinking. Now these people are telling me I really have underlying emotional problems. I hear all these generalizations being made, and every time I question one, it's like I'm criticizing motherhood and apple pie. I know I'm a drunk, but I'm not *that* foggy.

BEN   (angrily) Look, Ted, we've all been very patient with you, but you're starting to interfere with my serenity. These people are trying to *help* you, for God's sake. You are emotionally screwed up. You are in emotional *pain*. Can't you see that? It's not the drinking. That's just the tip of the iceberg.

TED   Bullshit.

BEN   Damn you, you stubborn jerk . . .

MARGARET   Ben, your blood pressure . . .

LEADER #2   Ted, I think perhaps you aren't ready for this group. Why don't you return to your room and talk to one of the staff? We can always start you in group in a few days. Ask for some medication if you need it to relax.

TED   My pleasure. I don't think a few days is going to change anything, though. (leaves room)

JANET   I am so embarrassed. Now you know what I put up with . . .

LEADER #2   Ted is in serious trouble, Janet. His denial, especially around his emotional defenses, is really formidable. It will take a lot of therapy to break through, and then probably years more of therapy to reconstruct his personality to a more mature level. I'd begin to question whether or not he's willing to submit to that kind of commitment . . . whether he's motivated enough to change. He seems to think his only problem is that he drinks too much.

JANET   I know. I've thought of divorcing him.

BEN   He's a hard nut to crack. A real intellectualizer.

JANET   Do you think maybe . . . well, I don't know, but . . . do you think maybe a program that was more focused on alcoholism rather than on emotions would be better for him?

LEADER #2   No. I think it would just reinforce his denial of his emotions. He might quit drinking, but he'd still be emotionally disturbed.

LEADER #1   Let us work on him for a few days. We may be able to break through his defenses.

LEADER #2   There's always a chance. And we hang on until they let go, you know.

JANET   Thank you. I feel better.

LEADER #1   Now about those sexual problems, Joe. Let's take a closer look at those issues of parenting you and your wife are dealing with . . .

JOE   Wait a minute. I've been sitting here thinking. I heard somewhere that you *can* be impotent after you quit drinking. I think it was in a magazine article. For a year, even, it said.

LEADER #1   That's not proven, Joe.

JOE   But if I'm having this problem only because I just quit drinking, after 20 years, then maybe it will go away by itself?

LEADER #1   You'll still have communication problems with your wife, Joe.

ELIZABETH   That's true. We'd still have the problem, Joe, even if our sex lives improved.

JOE   I understand that. But doesn't it make sense that if our sex lives improve, we'll feel better?

LEADER #2   Of course, but what's your point?

JOE   My point is that if Ted is right, and my problem is a result of drinking for 20 years, and will go away by itself in time, then isn't it wrong to blame it on arguments we have over who our son is dating?

LEADER #1   Don't you care about your son, Joe?

JOE   Of course, I do.

LEADER #1   Alcoholism is a family disease, Joe. You have to be sensitive to the needs and problems of those close to you, as well as to your own difficulties and desires.

JOE   I *know* that. But it's a separate problem.

MARGARET   There aren't any separate problems in families,
Joe. We're all part of a whole. Everything we do and say
affects others.

JOE   I don't think you all understand me.

BEN   I think that guy Ted got to you and mixed you all up.

LEADER #1   Did you identify with Ted, Joe?

JOE   No . . . well, a little. I've also wondered what all this
had to do with alcoholism. I mean, sometimes it seems as
though we spend all our time treating the family, when I'm
the one with the disease.

LEADER #2   Your family has a disease, too, Joe. Alcoholism
is a family disease.

JOE   Then how come I'm the only one in the hospital?

LEADER #2   That's the way society sees it, Joe. If your
insurance covered it, it would probably be a good idea to
put the whole family in the hospital.

JOE   Wait a minute, please. I went to a lecture today, where
the counselor told us that we suffered from a family disease, and in order to get better, everyone had to have
therapy, and family therapy especially. He said it was
impossible to recover unless we treated the whole family.

LEADER #1   That's right.

JOE   Well, there are three guys in my office who have been
in AA for a while, and they are all happy, and not a single
one knows what I'm talking about when I tell him about
this family therapy. One of them doesn't even *have* any
family, for Christ's sakes, and he's been sober for three
years.

LEADER #2   But are they really well, Joe? Or are they just
dry?

JOE   They *seem* fine.

LEADER #2   They're covering up, Joe. We've seen it time and
time again. Alcoholics stop drinking and don't deal with
their emotional lives. They end up on a dry drunk. They're
more unhappy than when they were drinking.

LEADER #1   Sometimes they get suicidal, Joe.

JOE   Are you saying that without this therapy, I might get
suicidal?

LEADER #2   It's a possibility, Joe. Unpleasant, but it must be faced.

ELIZABETH   Now you know why I insisted so hard that you stick with the program, Joe. Without their help, you could become depressed and kill yourself. They taught me that before I ever got you in here.

JOE   But they'd never even *met* me.

LEADER #1   Are you sure you've surrendered, Joe? Or are you still fighting the need for help?

LEADER #2   Perhaps that is why you relate so much to Ted. You too haven't surrendered.

JOE   No, I know I need help. But what Ted says made sense.

JANET   For God's sake, don't follow Ted.

JOE   Don't worry, I've come this far. I'll stick with the group.

LEADER #2   That's good, Joe. You're doing great.

JOE   Sure . . . except in bed.

LEADER #1   I'm sure we can solve that, Joe. Therapy will help you with that. It's probably just a psychological problem that will respond to treatment.

JOE   I hope so . . . because if this isn't physical, and it doesn't go away after all this talking, I really will want to kill myself.

LEADER #1   Don't worry, Joe. Now, let's get back to your relationship with your son, and these suspicions you have about the girl he's dating.

Bonding: _____

_____

Climate: _____

_____

Values: _____

_____

_____

Status and traditions: _____

_____

_____

Structure: _____

_____

Mentality: _____

_____

Dominant mode: _____

_____

Other modes during session: _____

_____

_____

Discussion

We should emphasize that we do not intend to criticize any
particular modality of therapy in these exercises. We make
such a disclaimer because, although this example illustrates
some of the really destructive features of the hopeful expectation mode, we don't want people to believe all family therapy
groups are like this. They most certainly are not.

Nonetheless, this exercise does show how the language of therapy can be used to fight the goals of change.

- *Bonding:* By the time Ted and Janet enter the group, it has already bonded firmly around a goal *other* than the treatment of alcoholism. Thus Ted's questions – quite reasonable in the light of his own goals for treatment – are actually a *threat* to the dominant agenda of the group, which is to maintain personal comfort.

  Ben and Margaret are the dominant "actives" characteristic of this mode. They collude with the leaders to suppress certain types of discussion. Janet fits in well with this active segment, but Joe is not so cooperative.

- *Climate:* There is a sense of fairly high morale in the foreground, with Ben and Margaret acting as cheerleaders for the group. However, the group's response to the questions raised by Ted and Joe belies this positivism.

- *Values:* This group encourages dependence on the designated leaders and on the group. It values quality of interaction *only* when the focus is on emotional issues. The actives seem to be willing to spend months or years in therapy – as approved by the leaders – working on problems *other* than alcoholism. Ted's desire to quit drinking and his willingness to identify himself as an alcoholic are of little importance to the group.

  Like other hopeful expectation groups, it also values recitation of the group's "party line" above intellectual inquiry. Thus generalizations, filled with jargon and intimations of superior wisdom, are offered to answer legitimate questions.

  When the group can't coerce Ted into compliance, he is excluded. When Joe shows signs of the same resistance, the coercive quality again surfaces – this time with success. Faith in the importance of the group's emotional and psychological preoccupations is valued above the needs of Joe and Ted, and indeed, of anyone who does not respond to the group's wisdom.

- *Status and traditions:* Again, here there are *two* groups. Joe, Ted, and perhaps any new member array on one side; they are dominated by an alliance between the "actives" and the two leaders.

- *Mentality:* "We know what is best, and it cannot be questioned."
- *Culture:* Struggle between the dominant "actives" and anyone who approaches recovery differently.

Alternative Interventions

Oddly enough, this particular group has many of the characteristics of the "sick" families it purports to treat. We would like to offer the hope that one or two simple changes could set this group on the road to work, but we would be lying. The best advice is to scrap this group, break up the alliance between the two leaders and their partnership with the Actives, and start all over, with an appropriate task.

GROUP PROCESS EXERCISE #7:
DEFENSE MECHANISM GROUP

Though most treatment groups deal extensively with defenses, this particular modality is specifically designed to teach addicts to recognize and point out defense mechanisms to one another as they appear during the course of the group. Leaders are instructed to maintain group boundaries and hold the group on task, but generally do little else. They *never* interact directly with the members.

In this example, there are six members and one leader. All are patients in an inpatient program.

LEADER   Our task for today is to study how defense mechanisms interfere with treatment of addictions.
(Group remains silent for several minutes.)
PERRY   Well? Isn't anyone going to start?
RUDY   Not me. I started last week.
PERRY   So can't you start this week?
RUDY   So why don't the therapists ever start the group? They're supposed to know what we're doing here.

JUNE   I agree. I don't see why everything around this place
is our responsibility.

RUDY   (to leader) Well? What do you say to that?

(no response from leader)

RUDY   Has anyone figured out why they won't answer direct
questions?

JUNE   It's against their rules.

RUDY   But *why?* Are these people insane?

PERRY   No. We are. Haven't you noticed?

RUDY   Seriously, I don't get the idea here. We're supposed to
have a group. But if we can't ask the leaders anything, how
are we supposed to know what to talk about?

JUNE   Talk about anything. What difference does it make?

RUDY   I don't want to waste time, you know.

JUNE   Well, to me, most of the stuff we do here is wasting
time.

PERRY   I know what you mean.

JUNE   So why do we put up with it? Why don't we leave?
What's keeping us in this joint?

RUDY   Fear of the alternative. There's a bench warrant
waiting for me.

PERRY   Drugs?

RUDY   Drugs.

PERRY   What a drag.

JUNE   Let's see if we can get this guy to talk.

(She reaches over and tweaks his knee. The leader doesn't
respond.)

JUNE   Nope. Dead to the world.

PERRY   Well, if they're not going to do something, then I
don't see how they can justify charging money for this
therapy.

JUNE   That's for damn sure.

RUDY   Why don't we just refuse to pay?

JUNE   That'll wake them up.

RUDY   If nobody paid, they'd sure as hell change their style
of therapy, wouldn't they?

PERRY   Either that or go under. (laughs)

JUNE   You guys notice how we're the only ones who ever
talk in this group?

PERRY   Yes. It's impossible to miss.

JUNE   What about you, Daniel? Or you, Lucy? Or Bobby? Don't you guys have something to say? No? . . . Figures.

RUDY   Well, we agree that the staff are a bunch of assholes. But what do we do with the rest of the hour?

JUNE   Is there any coffee around?

RUDY   No.

JUNE   Maybe I'll look for some.

PERRY   I'll go with you.

LEADER   Sounds like the group is willing to leave the room rather than work on its own.

JUNE   Would you look at that. The dead speak.

RUDY   He thinks we don't want to do any work.

JUNE   He's right. Nobody else in this group is doing anything. Why should I?

RUDY   Well, you want to get sober, don't you?

JUNE   Maybe, maybe not.

RUDY   You don't know?

JUNE   Do you?

RUDY   I *have* to. I'm in *big* trouble. My options are gone.

PERRY   So are mine. I have two drunk driving convictions, and another one coming to trial in a month. I'm looking at jail.

JUNE   So what? I've been in jail. And why get sober if they're just going to lock you up anyway?

RUDY   So you don't go out and get another one after you get released, right Perry?

PERRY   No bull. They are throwing the book at people like me.

JUNE   (to other group members) Any of you guys got any comments?

RUDY   Hey, we're talking about something.

JUNE   What?

RUDY   How to stay out of jail.

JUNE   Don't get touchy.

PERRY   The only way for me to stay out of jail is to stay away from drugs.

RUDY   Me, too. But I knew that before this last bust.

PERRY   Have you ever tried to stay clean?

RUDY   Sure, lots of times. But I always bullshit myself back into it.

PERRY   Like?

RUDY   One time I'd been clean for a month, and I convinced myself that I could *sell* drugs without using them. Get the gain without the pain, you know? Lasted about a week. Then another time, I got back together with an old lady of mine, who was using coke. I was going to rescue her, you know? Six weeks in the hospital down the drain.

LEADER   Those are defense mechanisms.

JUNE   What did he say?

PERRY   He said that Rudy was talking about defense mechanisms. Making excuses for his relapses.

JUNE   What the fuck does he know about it?

RUDY   Right. I mean, this dude won't even answer a simple question.

PERRY   You are using defense mechanisms, you know. Remember the lecture? When you told yourself you'd sell dope but not deal it, you were rationalizing.

RUDY   What?

PERRY   You wanted to sell the dope, right? Because you needed bread. So you knew that if you sold it, had it around the house, there was a chance you'd start using it. After all, you'd been strung out on it before. So you told yourself that you could somehow sell it without using it, even though you probably knew you couldn't. You rationalized it.

JUNE   But what about when he went back to his old lady?

PERRY   Same thing. He told himself that he could get her clean, when the truth was that she would get him dirty.

JUNE   Far out.

RUDY   I don't think it's true.

PERRY   Why not?

RUDY   I really *did* think I could deal without using.

PERRY   You don't *know* you're bullshitting yourself. You do it unconsciously.

JUNE   That's kind of neat.

RUDY   So what do I do about this?
PERRY   You look for defense mechanisms you used in this
group.
RUDY   I haven't used any.
LEADER   There were a number of defense mechanisms used
at the beginning of this group.
PERRY   Like when we said we couldn't do anything unless
they told us what to do.
JUNE   We could, couldn't we?
PERRY   Damn right we could.
JUNE   So were we rationalizing?
LEADER   The defense mechanism used there was externali-
zation.
PERRY   That I don't get. What's the difference between
rationalizing and externalizing?
JUNE   I haven't got an idea.
RUDY   They talked about it in that lecture.
JUNE   (to other members) Any of you remember?
BOBBY   No. Maybe it was that you blame things on other
people.
RUDY   That's it. We were saying that what we did depended
on what *they* did. Which wasn't true. What we do depends
on *us*.
PERRY   Right. That is true.
JUNE   This group is almost over, and I still don't get what
all these defense mechanisms are all about.
PERRY   So read the article they gave you.
JUNE   There was an article on this?
PERRY   Yeah.
RUDY   That must be a defense mechanism. She didn't even
look.
JUNE   I didn't think it was important.
PERRY   What if you were wrong? What if staying clean
depended on knowing this stuff?
JUNE   It doesn't.
PERRY   How do you know?
RUDY   I mean, how many times have you been in programs?
JUNE   Don't ask. Lots.

RUDY   So maybe you're still pretending what you do here isn't important.

LEADER   That is called minimizing.

RUDY   There you go. You are a minimizer.

PERRY   So now you got something to do before this next group.

JUNE   What?

RUDY   Learn the damn defense mechanisms, is what.

PERRY   You too, Rudy.

RUDY   And what about the rest of you guys?

BOBBY   I'll learn them.

PERRY   And if you don't, we're gonna tell you what defense mechanism that is, right, Rudy?

RUDY   You are gonna be off-task, all right.

Bonding: _____

_____

Climate: _____

_____

Values: _____

_____

_____

Status and traditions: _____

_____

_____

Structure: _____

_____

Mentality: _____

_____

Dominant mode: _____

_____

Other modes during session: _____

_____

_____

Discussion

Here is another example of a group as it passes through the helpless and hostile modes into work.

Interestingly, this leader's approach—he essentially *refuses* to lead the group, outside of giving the task—appears to be very effective with this set of members. Clearly, more active leadership would have allowed the group to remain dependent, rather than encouraging work.

- *Bonding:* At first, the group bonds negatively around the idea that responsibility is the leader's and that the members cannot accomplish anything on their own. Then members actually begin to leave the room, which provokes an observation from the leader that the group is actively avoiding work. Finally, the group bonds positively around the idea that they *can* learn to work on the task.
- *Climate:* Moves from passive cynicism and hostility to relatively high morale.
- *Values:* This group, like most, chooses to work in response to recognition of the seriousness of the situation. Asked his motive for sticking with treatment, one member responds, "fear of the alternative."

Once in the work mode, the group values the task. While in the helpless and hostile modes, the group characteristically values everything *but* the task.

• *Status:* The hostile group assigns status to June, who is the most critical and cynical member. The work group takes it back and assigns leadership to Perry, who seems to understand defense mechanisms better than the others.

• *Traditions:* This group is in the process of establishing some traditions of its own. For example, members seem ready to abandon for good the idea that beginning the group is the leader's responsibility. We would expect the next session to start easily, initiated by Perry or Rudy and on task from the start. If a newcomer asks about the leader's strange passivity, he'll probably be told that "this is just the way our group works."

• *Mentality:* Shifts from "we don't know what to do with ourselves" (helpless mode) to "this is totally unfair" (hostile mode) and finally stabilizes as "now let's get to work on defense mechanisms."

• *Culture:* Shifts from a struggle against the leader and the task to a struggle between any member who resists work and the rest of the group.

Alternative Interventions

This group is essentially on target by session's end, so few changes are necessary. The single most important reason for its success is the leader's ability to resist assuming control in the early moments of the session, when the group was floundering. Had he given in, the group would have fallen into an easy dependence and eventually become stuck in the hopeful expectation mode.

CHAPTER 6

CREATING AN EFFECTIVE ADDICTIONS GROUP

THERAPISTS HAVE TRADITIONALLY assumed that a solid background in mental health models is adequate preparation for leading addictions groups. Nothing could be further from the truth. In fact, an approach that creates a "good" mental health group may render that group virtually impotent with alcoholics and drug addicts.

Psychodynamic exploration—which, when all is said and done, is still the main focus of the mental health model—is usually inappropriate with addicts. Thus groups that rely primarily on psychodynamic insight flounder. This is because recovery from addiction involves, first and foremost, changes in behavior. Alcoholics Anonymous has a slogan for the newcomer: "Bring the body and the mind will follow." Most mental health groups take the opposite tack, trying to change the way the patient feels in order to motivate abstinence. Is it realistic to expect an alcoholic or addict to accurately assess and treat his own addiction while his brain is still under the influence?

Some psychodynamically oriented mental health groups devote considerable energy to uncovering the "underlying" causes" of the members' drug use. But once again, everything we know about addiction as a disease advises us that no such etiology exists; even if it did, its relevance to the present dilemma would be questionable. Alcoholics and addicts use drugs for a variety of reasons, become addicted, and then have a hell of a time stopping. The struggle to recover is made no less painful by the fact that you've recalled your long-ago motives for experimenting with chemicals. And you're every bit as addicted as you were before you learned this information.

In Table 1 we compare addictions groups and those found in traditional mental health programs.

As you can see, these two groups are really animals of wholly different breeds. As we mentioned earlier, alcoholism treatment groups have more in common with medical rehabilitation groups than with psychotherapy.

Nevertheless, much leadership training devotes itself to teaching counselors to operate the *wrong kind of groups* for these patients. Many therapeutic "problems," we imagine, arise from this confusion. The designated leader may well have been trained to lead in such a way as to sabotage the goals of the group.

KEYS TO STRUCTURING ADDICTIONS GROUPS

1. *The group should complement the self-help fellowship, rather than serve as an alternative.*

Self-help groups – principally Twelve Step fellowships – offer a number of advantages to the newly sober person. They're widely available; they're free; they meet at convenient times in convenient locations; there are many meetings to choose from; you can attend as often as you wish for as long as you wish. Professional treatment cannot match these services, nor should it try.

Thus it makes sense for the professionally led group to focus on getting the patient to the point where he or she is capable of making productive use of such fellowships. That means helping alcoholics or addicts overcome whatever difficulties they encounter – from shyness to fear of speaking in large groups to transportation problems. Remember: the point of treatment is to help the alcoholic establish a program for remaining sober long after his term in group is completed. When you're no long-

TABLE 1

MENTAL HEALTH GROUP	ADDICTIONS TREATMENT GROUP
1. Many different *goals* exist within the group. Each member may desire and strive for something different from others.	1. Group members tend to have the same primary goal: recovery from alcoholism.
2. Due to the disparity of goals, the group has many tasks: to help John with job search, Judy with anxiety, Joe with sex problems, Harold with his "voices," etc. Thus discussion frequently applies to only *some* of the members present.	2. Group tends to have one dominant task; it devotes its time to the common problem of establishing stable recovery.
3. Few rules, since members' needs vary and goals differ. Thus flexibility is prized and the structure accommodates a variety of activities within the group.	3. Here there may be many rules, reflecting the commonality of purpose and the ways in which the structure must support the common goal.
4. Obviously, these groups are often fairly unorganized, and lateness, etc., is often tolerated.	4. Because of the need for results, these groups are usually quite organized.
5. Usually, members are encouraged—sometimes even pushed—to express personal feelings. This is regarded as *essential* to progress.	5. Since members' goals are more behavioral than strictly emotional, expression of feeling is not given the high priority it is given in the mental health group.

er in his life, where will he go and what will he do to avoid relapse?

This is where so many therapists go astray. They offer their group as an option to AA or NA and attract people who resist attending these self-help groups. Soon enough they discover that their success rate is low and their group has become a holding facility for chronic recidivists.

2. *Provide the same education for each member.*

The first barrier to recovery is the addict's profound ignorance of the nature of his or her disease. We recommend that leaders provide essential information – in the form of reading, films, lectures, etc. – outside the session, to avoid wasting vast chunks of group time on didactic education. This can be as simple as assigning relevant articles or books, or as complex as the "school for sobriety" we developed for our own treatment programs. Both serve the same function: They standardize the fund of knowledge within the group. That makes it easier to communicate.

3. *Make abstinence a prerequisite for participation.*

If you're treating addicts in an inpatient setting, this is no problem. But in an outpatient group – whether composed of people who have completed inpatient treatment and are now in aftercare or of people who have always been outpatients – it's an entirely different matter. We've noticed that some therapists attempt to treat addiction while the patient is still drinking or using drugs, either daily or between sessions. The group takes upon itself the burden of convincing the alcoholic to give up alcohol and of supporting him or her in efforts to avoid the next drink.

This is a terrible thing to do to an outpatient group. There is nothing which interferes with the work mode more effectively than relapsing members. Their presence turns the session into a support or confrontation group for one or two people and leads to neglect of the very real needs of those who are managing to stay sober.

As we've previously discussed, alcoholism is *not* a "psychological" disorder, and treatment is only secondarily psychosocial in orientation. The baseline treatment for any alcoholic is ongoing abstinence from alcohol and similar drugs. What we tend to identify as treatment is really *support* for the alcoholic in his struggle to establish stable abstinence. But such support is largely ineffective unless the alcoholic stops drinking. A group that attempts to treat alcoholics who have not stopped drinking is not treating alcoholism. Such a group may be treating alcoholics, but it is not making inroads into their disease.

Therefore, we recommend that therapists make use of inpatient or structured outpatient programs designed to do what the lone therapist often cannot: free the alcoholic from the cycle of drinking and withdrawal. Once the alcoholic is committed to remaining abstinent, treatment can be of some value to him.

Just as counselors sometimes forget this simple truth, so too do alcoholics. One of our patients once approached us with the confession that he still drank between sessions.

"I've definitely felt less depressed since I joined this group," he confided, "but about once or twice a week, I still get a craving for a drink. I managed to control it on Tuesday – only had a few beers, and stopped on my own, no problem – but I kind of blew it on Friday. One of the guys in this group saw me buying booze, so I figured I'd better tell you so you wouldn't hear it on the grapevine and get the wrong idea. I really want to stop this, and I think I'm doing a lot better, but I guess I'm not all the way clear of the drinking yet."

As he turned to go, we stopped him. "Where do you think you're going?" we said.

"Into the session," he replied.

"That group is for people who've stopped drinking and want to *stay* stopped. *You* haven't stopped drinking yet. We'd recommend you try detox or an inpatient program. That's where people go when they can't stop by themselves."

"What?" he said angrily, "I *told* you I'm getting better."

"You're wrong," we replied, "You're getting worse. You've completely missed the point of treatment, and you need to start all over and get it right."

"Suppose I refuse to go into the hospital?" he challenged.

"Hey, that's up to you," we told him, "but you can't go into the group, either."

"I can't believe this," he continued, "I was *honest* with you, and you reward me by throwing me out of the group."

"Correction," we told him, "we are simply directing you to treatment which will work, instead of allowing you to waste time in a treatment group which isn't doing you much good. If you get sober, you can re-enroll in the group. And we don't have to reward you for honesty. Honesty is its own reward, as the saying goes."

"This is ridiculous," he came back, trying to get the last word. "I might as well go and drink."

"Hey, you are already doing *that*," we advised him, "So it won't represent any great change."

That alcoholic, by the way, went on a three-week binge, after which he checked into a treatment program. He's been sober more than five years now. We think we saved him a year of absolutely fruitless therapy, which would have been punctuated by relapses and increasing depression.

He may still think we're the meanest SOB's in the helping professions, but after all, this isn't a popularity contest, is it?

The Role of Feelings

One area where we differ substantially from the mental health models is in our approach to the expression of feelings within the group.

It seems to us that much of the emotional baggage which accompanies alcoholism is really the result of the alcoholic's own misconception about what is wrong with him.

Like most Americans, drinking alcoholics have been taught that alcoholism is a sign of personal weakness, irresponsibility, emotional repression, psychological inadequacy, stress, or childhood discontent—in other words, everything *but* a chronic, progressive, physiological disease.

Thus alcoholics spend years misinterpreting their own behavior and experience. This is reinforced by the fact that just about everybody they happen to know and love – family, employers, coworkers, friends, and distant relatives – also misinterprets these same symptoms in different ways. The resulting syndrome of misinterpretation and misperception is about as difficult to break as the alcoholic's addiction to alcohol. The only really effective solution is to change the alcoholic's attitude towards his own disease.

Recognizing that the bulk of alcoholics' negative feelings about themselves are the direct and indirect results of their negative attitude towards having this disease, we strive to change these feelings by changing this attitude. We change their attitude by changing the information they receive, and we change this information through a process of *education*. To simplify: we don't devote time and energy to "uncovering" the reasons that individuals with five- or ten- or twenty-year histories of alcoholism feel bad about themselves. We *know* why they feel bad. We want to *change* that feeling, and we believe that is done through education.

Thus we avoid concentrating on feelings in group because:

1. the alcoholic's augmented nervous system tends to exaggerate emotional responses to any situation;
2. the alcoholic's feelings often result from defense mechanisms that should be examined and penetrated, not given credence as legitimate; and
3. expression of feelings in and of itself does little to advance the goals of treatment.

Instead, we concentrate on *changing* feelings by changing behavior and attitude.

STRUCTURING A GROUP FOR MAXIMUM EFFECTIVENESS

The *structure*, you will recall, is the how, when, where, etc. of the group. Here are some suggestions for making the group's structure fit the needs of alcoholism treatment:

1. *Group size:* Maintain a group of between five and twelve members.
2. *Homogeneity:* Make sure all patients have essentially the same diagnosis – alcoholism or addiction – and the same goal.
3. *Boundaries:*
   Time: Make sure the group starts and ends on time. Don't allow the group to establish its own "standard time," which means that members always arrive ten minutes after the designated starting time or run ten minutes over the group's supposed end.
   Place: Find an environment conducive to working on the task. There is a lot of mythology in this area. For a while, we were all taught that you can't have a group with a table in the center of the room, because the table "inhibited" free discussion. We don't agree. Make sure that room temperature is comfortable, noise and interruptions are minimal, and issues such as smoking are dealt with to the group's satisfaction.
   Task: Give the group a task – a topic related to the advancement of the four goals of treatment – prior to the group. Encourage members to think about what they want to do before they arrive. Do not worry about spontaneity. This is not a psychotherapy group.
   Roles: Let the group assign roles as indicated. Group members should be encouraged to assume leadership and responsibility functions and to make their own mistakes. The designated leader is then free to fill functions that the group is *not* meeting on its own. Try to maintain a "consultant" status within the group and dodge members who try to cast you into a rigid role.

Remember, too, that unlike typical psychotherapy patients, addictions patients view their participation as *involuntary.* Some type of "gun" – be it medical, legal, financial, marital, occupational, or actual – is making them seek help. Thus, relying on them to search for psychodynamic insight or to "work" in an environment that does not strongly *encourage* that behavior is probably futile. As with all resistant patients, the group must be structured to direct them towards work.

SOME TYPICAL ADDICTIONS TREATMENT GROUPS

Below we describe some of the groups we conduct in our inpatient and outpatient treatment programs. It's important to remember that these groups are designed specifically for people in the first few months of sobriety. However, some of the groups we favor—such as the defense mechanism study group—are well suited to later stages of recovery. Others, such as the self-diagnosis group, are of value principally in the first weeks of treatment.

Self-Diagnosis Group

• *Task:* Review the symptoms of addictive disease that group members have experienced.
• *Average group size:* Six to eight members; one leader.
• *Goal:* To facilitate self-diagnosis for individual members.
• *Materials:* Members are all given copies of a curve indicating the course of progression and recovery from their disease and information about the symptoms of addictive diseases. They may bring this information to the group and refer to it as they participate in the discussion.
    The "bell curves" for assisting self-diagnosis (see Figures 1, 2, and 3) are found, in one version or another, in just about every treatment program we've encountered. We include them purely as examples of materials used in treatment today.
• *Leader's role:* This group often features fairly active leadership, since most members are new and defense mechanisms and toxicity may be pronounced. The leader may do some teaching in the group. As information within the group accumulates, the leader turns active leadership over to more advanced members.

    EXAMPLE

LEADER   The task of this group is to review the symptoms of addiction and alcoholism that members of this group have experienced.

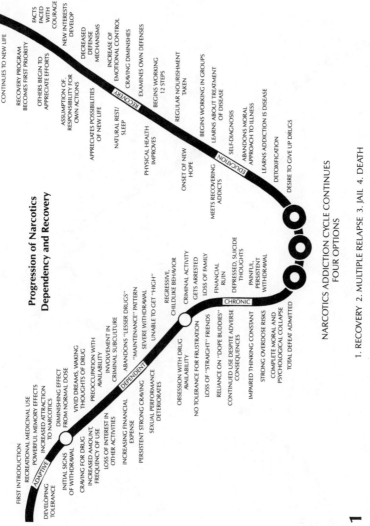

Progression of Narcotics Dependency and Recovery

FIRST INTRODUCTION
RECREATIONAL MEDICINAL USE
POWERFUL MEMORY EFFECTS
INCREASED ATTRACTION TO NARCOTICS
DIMINISHING EFFECT FROM NORMAL DOSE

DEVELOPING TOLERANCE

INITIAL SIGNS OF WITHDRAWAL

ADAPTIVE

VIVID DREAMS, WAKING THOUGHTS OF DRUG
CRAVING FOR DRUG
INCREASED AMOUNT, FREQUENCY OF USE
PREOCCUPATION WITH AVAILABILITY
LOSS OF INTEREST IN OTHER ACTIVITIES
INVOLVEMENT IN CRIMINAL SUBCULTURE
INCREASING FINANCIAL EXPENSE
ABANDONS "LESSER DRUGS"
PERSISTENT STRONG CRAVING
"MAINTENANCE" PATTERN
SEXUAL PERFORMANCE DETERIORATES
SEVERE WITHDRAWAL
UNABLE TO GET "HIGH"

DEPENDENT

REGRESSIVE, CHILDLIKE BEHAVIOR
OBSESSION WITH DRUG AVAILABILITY
CRIMINAL ACTIVITY
NO TOLERANCE FOR FRUSTRATION
GETS ARRESTED
LOSS OF "STRAIGHT" FRIENDS
LOSS OF FAMILY
RELIANCE ON "DOPE BUDDIES"
FINANCIAL RUIN
CONTINUED USE DESPITE ADVERSE CONSEQUENCES
DEPRESSED, SUICIDE THOUGHTS
IMPAIRED THINKING CONSTANT
STRONG OVERDOSE RISKS
PAINFUL, PERSISTENT WITHDRAWAL
COMPLETE MORAL AND PSYCHOLOGICAL COLLAPSE
TOTAL DEFEAT ADMITTED

CHRONIC

DESIRE TO GIVE UP DRUGS
DETOXIFICATION
LEARNS ADDICTION IS DISEASE
ABANDONS MORAL APPROACH TO ILLNESS
SELF-DIAGNOSIS
LEARNS ABOUT TREATMENT OF DISEASE
BEGINS WORKING IN GROUPS
MEETS RECOVERING ADDICTS

EDUCATION

ONSET OF NEW HOPE
REGULAR NOURISHMENT TAKEN
PHYSICAL HEALTH IMPROVES
BEGINS WORKING 12 STEPS
EXAMINES OWN DEFENSES
CRAVING DIMINISHES
NATURAL REST/ SLEEP
INCREASE OF EMOTIONAL CONTROL
APPRECIATES POSSIBILITIES OF NEW LIFE
DECREASED DEFENSE MECHANISMS
ASSUMPTION OF RESPONSIBILITY FOR OWN ACTIONS
NEW INTERESTS DEVELOP
OTHERS BEGIN TO APPRECIATE EFFORTS
RECOVERY PROGRAM BECOMES FIRST PRIORITY

RECOVERY

CONTINUES TO NEW LIFE
FACTS FACED WITH COURAGE

NARCOTICS ADDICTION CYCLE CONTINUES
FOUR OPTIONS

1. RECOVERY 2. MULTIPLE RELAPSE 3. JAIL 4. DEATH

Figure 1

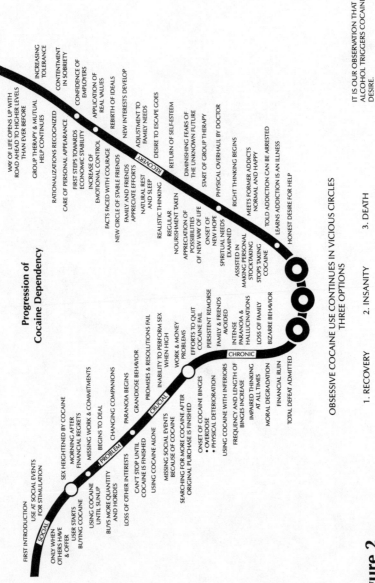

Progression of Cocaine Dependency

SOCIAL

- FIRST INTRODUCTION
- USE AT SOCIAL EVENTS FOR STIMULATION
- ONLY WHEN OTHERS HAVE & OFFER
- USER STARTS BUYING COCAINE
- SEX HEIGHTENED BY COCAINE
- MORNING AFTER FINANCIAL REGRETS

PROBLEM

- USING COCAINE UNTIL SUNUP
- BUYS MORE QUANTITY AND HORDES
- MISSING WORK & COMMITMENTS
- BEGINS TO DEAL
- LOSS OF OTHER INTERESTS
- CHANGING COMPANIONS
- PARANOIA BEGINS

CRUCIAL

- CAN'T STOP UNTIL COCAINE IS FINISHED
- GRANDIOSE BEHAVIOR
- USING COCAINE ALONE
- PROMISES & RESOLUTIONS FAIL
- MISSING SOCIAL EVENTS BECAUSE OF COCAINE
- INABILITY TO PERFORM SEX WHEN HIGH
- SEARCHING FOR MORE COCAINE AFTER ORIGINAL PURCHASE IS FINISHED
- WORK & MONEY PROBLEMS
- ONSET OF COCAINE BINGES
  - OVERDOSE
  - PHYSICAL DETERIORATION
- EFFORTS TO QUIT COCAINE FAIL
- PERSISTENT REMORSE
- USING COCAINE WITH INFERIORS
- FAMILY & FRIENDS AVOIDED
- FREQUENCY AND LENGTH OF BINGES INCREASE
- INTENSE PARANOIA & HALLUCINATIONS

CHRONIC

- IMPAIRED THINKING AT ALL TIMES
- LOSS OF FAMILY
- BIZARRE BEHAVIOR
- MORAL DEGRADATION
- FINANCIAL RUIN
- TOTAL DEFEAT ADMITTED

OBSESSIVE COCAINE USE CONTINUES IN VICIOUS CIRCLES
THREE OPTIONS

1. RECOVERY   2. INSANITY   3. DEATH

- HONEST DESIRE FOR HELP
- LEARNS ADDICTION IS AN ILLNESS
- TOLD ADDICTION CAN BE ARRESTED
- MEETS FORMER ADDICTS NORMAL AND HAPPY
- RIGHT THINKING BEGINS
- ASSISTED IN MAKING PERSONAL STOCKTAKING
- STOPS TAKING COCAINE
- PHYSICAL OVERHAUL BY DOCTOR
- SPIRITUAL NEEDS EXAMINED
- START OF GROUP THERAPY
- ONSET OF NEW HOPE
- DIMINISHING FEARS OF THE UNKNOWN FUTURE
- APPRECIATION OF POSSIBILITIES OF NEW WAY OF LIFE

RECOVERY

- REGULAR NOURISHMENT TAKEN
- RETURN OF SELF-ESTEEM
- NATURAL REST AND SLEEP
- DESIRE TO ESCAPE GOES
- REALISTIC THINKING
- ADJUSTMENT TO FAMILY NEEDS
- FAMILY AND FRIENDS APPRECIATE EFFORTS
- NEW INTERESTS DEVELOP
- NEW CIRCLE OF STABLE FRIENDS
- REBIRTH OF IDEALS
- FACTS FACED WITH COURAGE
- APPLICATION OF REAL VALUES
- INCREASE OF EMOTIONAL CONTROL
- CONFIDENCE OF EMPLOYERS
- CARE OF PERSONAL APPEARANCE
- FIRST STEPS TOWARDS ECONOMIC STABILITY
- RATIONALIZATIONS RECOGNIZED
- CONTENTMENT IN SOBRIETY
- GROUP THERAPY & MUTUAL HELP CONTINUES
- INCREASING TOLERANCE
- WAY OF LIFE OPENS UP WITH ROAD AHEAD TO HIGHER LEVELS THAN EVER BEFORE

IT IS OUR OBSERVATION THAT ALCOHOL TRIGGERS COCAINE DESIRE.

Figure 2

The Progression and Recovery of the ALCOHOLIC in the Disease of Alcoholism

To be read from left to right.

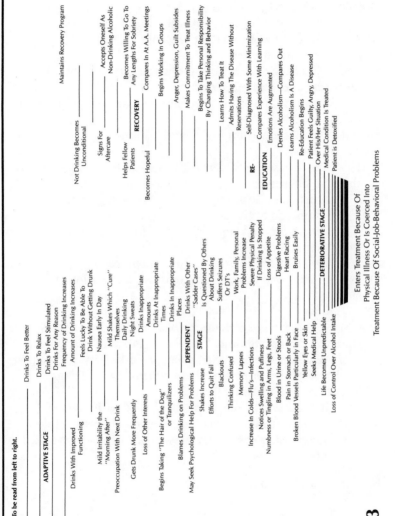

Figure 3

JOE   Well, I don't think I *am* an alcoholic, so there's nothing
to review.

FRANK   Then why are you here?

JOE   I was sick. I couldn't eat right, and I wasn't sleeping.

TOM   Why'd they put you in the alcohol unit, though?

JOE   I don't know why.

FRANK   Did the doctor say that he thought your physical
problems were related to drinking?

JOE   He said maybe they were, but he didn't sound positive
to me.

FRANK   You know drinking causes insomnia.

JOE   It does?

TOM   And stomach problems. I had them for two years, and
thought I had stomach cancer. It was the booze.

JOE   Didn't the doctor tell you that at the beginning?

TOM   I didn't go to the doctor. I diagnosed myself as suffering from cancer, and kept drinking. If I had cancer, why
worry about alcohol?

JOE   Wow. But I didn't drink that much, really.

FRANK   You don't always have to drink a whole lot to get
sick.

JOE   What?

FRANK   You can get sick even when you're drinking less
than you did at one time. I used to drink a fifth of whiskey
every day, and never missed a day of work. Now, I end up in
the hospital five days after I start drinking, and a pint
knocks me on my tail.

JOE   No kidding? I can't drink like I used to, either.

FRANK   That's a symptom of alcoholism. Decreased tolerance. Look at the sheet they gave you, with the curve on it.
You'll see it on there.

Step Discussion Group

• *Task:* To discuss a given step from AA's Twelve Step program.
• *Average group size:* Six to twelve members; one leader.
• *Goal:* To familiarize members with the use of the steps in
establishing stable sobriety.

- *Materials: AA's Twelve Steps and Twelve Traditions*, which reviews the steps from the perspective of the early members of AA, and *The Twelve Steps Revisited*, which discusses the steps from the perspective of the chronic disease model of alcoholism. Members read selections on the chosen step prior to attending the group.
- *Leader's role:* Leaders are fairly passive in this group, allowing members to discuss the step in any way they choose. The leadership functions center mainly on compromising and on reconciling differences as the group struggles with typical issues of conflict for newly recovering alcoholics, such as the existence and usefulness of the Higher Power. Leader holds task boundaries while encouraging the group to set and hold its own task boundaries.

EXAMPLE

WAYNE   I don't think I can use the program of AA, and especially, I can't use the second step. It's against my religion.

SUSAN   What? How on earth did you arrive at that conclusion?

WAYNE   Well, I was raised a Roman Catholic. And one of the Ten Commandments says that you shouldn't put any God before the God of the Church.

DAVID   So what?

WAYNE   Well, last week you all told me that in AA, the Higher Power doesn't have to be God, it can be the AA group, or your sponsor, or even the table, if you want. But it doesn't have to be God.

SUSAN   Yeah, that's right.

WAYNE   Well, if I follow that, and make AA my Higher Power, I'll go to Hell because I'll break that commandment. I'll be putting AA before the God of the Church.

SUSAN   You're kidding.

WAYNE   No, I'm serious. So I'll go to AA, but I just don't feel I can work on the steps, because it's against my religion.

SUSAN   How long did it take to think of this argument?

WAYNE   I've been thinking about it for quite a while. But it germinated into its present form last night.

SUSAN   That is the single strangest example of rationalizing I have ever in my life heard. You can't work the steps because if you do you'll go to Hell.

DAVID   Wayne, we didn't say you *had* to use AA as your Higher Power. It's perfectly all right to use God, you know.

WAYNE   But if other people can use AA instead of God, they're still breaking the commandment. So AA is wrong when it tells them to use AA as a Higher Power.

DAVID   Wayne, AA doesn't tell anybody to do anything. They just make *suggestions*. You take the advice or leave it, whatever you want. You can use AA as your HP, or God, or whatever. The third step says, "as we understood Him." *You* get to choose the meaning of God for yourself.

WAYNE   Oh. But what about those other people in AA, who use AA or a table or whatever as the Higher Power. I mean, they're all going to Hell. Shouldn't we try to do something for them?

DAVID   Let's let *them* worry about that, Wayne. It's a selfish program.

Defense Mechanism Study Group

- *Task:* To study defense mechanisms as they are used in the group.
- *Average size:* Eight to twelve members; one or two leaders.
- *Goal:* To give members experience in identifying and pointing out defense mechanisms as they occur.
- *Materials:* Each member is given reference materials (see Table 2) on various defense mechanisms and brings the material to the session.
- *Leader's role:* This group has a strong *experiential* focus. Members are given the task of identifying defenses, not only in their past behavior, but also as they are used by other members during the session. Remember that we're not aware of our own psychological defenses until after the fact—usual-

TABLE 2
DEFENSE MECHANISMS

Defense mechanisms are unconscious psychological devices which we use to protect ourselves from those aspects of reality which we do not wish to face. By employing defense mechanisms, we avoid looking at issues which might cause us worry or anxiety. Defense mechanisms are used by everyone in many different areas of everyday life. In the development of an addictive disease, however, an excessive or pathological reliance on defense mechanisms appears, which in turn "blinds" the addicted person to the extent and severity of his or her illness. This effectively prolongs the dangerous phase of the disease by preventing the addicted person from understanding the need to seek treatment.

Even after the addicted person stops drinking/drugging, defense mechanisms often lead him into relapse. By employing them he may justify behaviors and decisions, such as the use of cross-addictive drugs, or stopping AA/NA/CA attendance, which contribute directly to his own failure.

Because of this, we have included a "Defense Mechanisms Study Group" in the program. Its task: to point out defense mechanisms as they occur within the group. To get maximum benefit from this group, we recommend the following:

1. Learn the defense mechanisms on this sheet (and their meanings) prior to this group.
2. Point out any defense mechanisms you observe others using during the group.
3. Accept feedback from others about defense mechanisms you are using.
4. Examine how those defense mechanisms might interfere with treatment, or lead to relapse.

Remember that defense mechanisms are used not to deceive others, but to deceive ourselves. Since we are not aware we are using them, we often become angry or defensive when others point this out to us. Nevertheless, if we are ever to understand our own behavior, we need to be told when we are relying on defense mechanisms rather than effective problem-solving methods. Here, then, are the defense mechanisms:

(continued)

TABLE 2 (continued)

DENIAL:
Individual avoids a painful or anxiety-producing situation by
"blinding" himself to its existence. May insist that a given fact "just
can't be true," despite evidence to the contrary. Example #1:
"Officer, my BAL just couldn't be that high—I haven't touched a
drop all day!" Example #2: "I don't care what you say about my
needing treatment! I know myself, and I can stop on my own!"
RATIONALIZATION:
Providing "explanations" to excuse inconsistent or irrational
behavior. If the person is aware his behavior is irrational, yet makes
excuses for it anyway, we say he is "alibiing." If he believes his own
excuses, he is "rationalizing." Example #1: "I know I got drunk and
made a fool of myself last night, but here's why . . . " Example #2:
"I know I should go to aftercare, but I just can't because. . . . "
MINIMIZING:
Protecting yourself from worry or anxiety about a problem by
making it seem less important than it is. Example #1: "I know I've
had blackouts, but not really that often . . . " Example #2: "I know
it's risky for me to live with my cocaine-using husband, but he
really isn't using that much lately . . . "
EXTERNALIZATION:
Acting as though outside forces/circumstances cause us to behave in
self-destructive ways. Believing this, we do not have to take responsibility for our own behavior. Example #1: "I got drunk because she
wouldn't stop nagging me." Example #2: "If my husband hadn't
died, I never would have become an alcoholic." Example #3: "I was
going to NA, but my ride got high, so I had to drop out myself."
INTELLECTUALIZATION:
The use of lengthy argument or small detail to distract from the task
at hand. Example #1: "Yes, I know my wife says I get drunk every
night, but let's discuss precisely what we mean by the term 'drunk.'"
Example #2: "My bathroom hasn't been cleaned by the housekeep-
er in three days. This can't be much of a treatment program, if you
can't even keep the bathrooms clean."
UNDOING:
Behavior which is designed to atone for previous unacceptable
actions. Example: Husband brings flowers to wife to make up for a
cocaine binge over the weekend. Wife cooks a big meal and plans a

quiet evening at home to make up for a weekend of drinking and fighting.

PROJECTION:

Projecting one's own undesirable traits or thoughts onto other people. It is destructive to relationships, since it encourages isolation and unreasonable suspicion. Example #1: "I know you people think I'll get drunk as soon as I leave." Example #2: "I stopped going to CA because I just knew that people there couldn't accept me."

PASSIVE NEGATIVISM:

Passively resists doing what is required. Procrastinates, "forgets," or remains "confused," thus preventing completion of treatment goals. Example #1: "I know I've been here three weeks, but I just can't remember if I had anything left to do on my treatment plan, and I can't seem to find it anyway." Example #2: "Yeah, I know I have to go to AA meetings, but can't I start tomorrow night? There's a good show on TV this evening."

ACTIVE NEGATIVISM:

Actively resists treatment. Refuses to take steps necessary to recover. Example: Attends group, but refuses to speak; completes inpatient program, but refuses aftercare. When he uses narcotics again says: "Sure, I know I'm going to get in trouble, but I just don't care."

DISPLACEMENT:

Redirecting emotions towards ideas, objects, or persons other than their legitimate source. Example #1: Alcoholic upset with himself for losing job, picks argument with wife over raising children. Source of much "perfectionism" and intolerance. Example #2: Patient, uncomfortable because of withdrawal, loses patience with nurse who is trying to help and accuses her of "driving him crazy."

FANTASY:

Escape from unpleasant situation through daydreaming or not paying attention. Example: Gazing out window during lecture to avoid hearing about medical consequences of drinking/drugging.

REGRESSION:

Return to less mature level of behavior. Example #1: Relapsing after a period of abstinence because somebody offended you. Example # 2: Coping with upcoming discharge by going to bed and refusing to attend meetings.

ly when we're suffering the consequences or when others are pointing out the error of our ways. The defense mechanism group simply allows us to understand our defenses even as we experience them. Members discuss important topics in a setting where other members are given the task of recognizing and pointing out denial, rationalization, externalizing, minimizing, etc., *as they happen.* This inevitably produces some degree of conflict and anxiety, and the leader must accordingly adopt a passive stance—refusing to answer direct questions, addressing all comments to the group rather than individuals, insisting that members interact with each other rather than with the leader. The advantage? This group—perhaps more than any other—can produce insight into the thinking patterns that promote and protect relapse, and can, if used correctly, illustrate graphically why *encouraging and accepting feedback from others* is so important in recovery from addiction.

EXAMPLE

DENNIS   So that's why I drank—I rationalized using alcohol because my girlfriend dumped me. I really was in a lot of pain, but I could have found some other outlet.

LYNN   I've been through that too. There's nothing worse than having your face rubbed in the dirt by somebody you thought cared about you.

VINCE   Personally, I think getting drunk and winding up in detox is worse.

DENNIS   I don't know about that. I think the emotional pain is awful. I think most people in my situation would have done the same thing.

VINCE   Now you're rationalizing again. You're blaming your relapse on circumstances.

DENNIS   I know that—didn't you just hear me say that? Where were you—asleep?

VINCE   No, I understood what you said. But I think you're still rationalizing. In your mind, getting drunk when somebody treats you badly is perfectly OK.

DENNIS   I don't think it's OK. I know I shouldn't have
gotten drunk. I don't understand why you're making such a
big deal out of this, anyway. It was only a weekend, for
Christ's sake.

VINCE   Now you're minimizing.

DENNIS   I am not.

LYNN   Yes you are. You make it sound like it was OK because you were only drunk for a weekend. But I happen to
know the only reason you stopped is because you got
picked up for DWI. If it hadn't been for that, you'd probably still be on a binge.

DENNIS   All right, all right, I give up. You win. I was
rationalizing, and minimizing, and whatever else you say. I
know what I did was wrong, and I learned my lesson. So
give it a rest, will you? It won't happen again.

LYNN   Isn't that denial? I mean, what would prevent it from
happening again? What makes you think you won't do the
exact same thing the next time?

DENNIS   I understand what I did wrong. People will tell me
if I'm getting into that way of thinking again.

MARTHA   You seem so defensive, though. If I was your
friend and I saw you setting yourself up for a relapse, I
don't know if I could bring myself to tell you, knowing how
mad you would get.

DENNIS   Of course I'm defensive. And you would be too, if
somebody was attacking you.

VINCE   Well, that's externalizing, I think. See, Dennis, the
point is that you take any kind of feedback as criticism. So
you're going to get mad whenever anybody tells you
something you don't want to hear. Which means no one will
confront you, you'll be on your own, and unless some
miracle occurs, will probably talk yourself into another
relapse in the near future. That's the problem, and that's
what you have to change.

CHAPTER 7

THE ART OF
LEADERSHIP

AS FAR AS WE'RE CONCERNED, effective group leadership consists of two simple but crucial activities. They are:

1. Helping the group get into the work mode, and
2. Once it's there, facilitating the work.

Anyone who adequately performs these functions will be a successful leader of a successful group.

No special knowledge of psychodynamics is required. Thus, an alcoholism counselor may be as effective as a social worker, a minister as a psychologist, a cardiologist as a psychiatrist, when it comes to leading addictions groups. Good leadership is a matter of getting results, not of understanding the psychological or emotional development of individual members.

Let's examine some of the techniques that used to accomplish our two goals.

DEALING WITH THE HELPLESS MODE

You will recall that helpless groups assume that the leader, rather than the group, is responsible for the success or failure of the session. To pull the group out of this mode, the leader must confront this underlying assumption.

MEMBER #1   Are we just going to sit here silently? Isn't the Leader supposed to start the group?

MEMBER #2   Well, *I* sure don't know what to do.

MEMBER #1   (to leader): We just don't understand. What are
we supposed to do?

LEADER   I thought I gave the task for the group just a few
minutes ago. It involved discussing the defense mechanisms you all have used, either to protect your drinking or
to avoid treating your disease.

MEMBER #1   Yeah, but we don't know how to do that.

LEADER   The members of this group don't know what the
defense mechanisms are?

MEMBER #1   No.

LEADER   Weren't you all in the class I taught yesterday on
defense mechanisms?

MEMBER #1   I guess so. But there was too much stuff to
remember.

LEADER   Doesn't anyone in the group recall the definitions
of denial and rationalization?

MEMBER #2   I remember we talked about them, but I had
just gotten a bad phone call from my wife about some
overdue bills, so I couldn't concentrate on the lecture.

LEADER   How about anyone else? Can anybody explain the
defenses to the group?

(silence)

LEADER   (sighs) Well, I guess we'll just have to sit here for
the remainder of the hour and contemplate our navels.

MEMBER #1   What do you mean? We told you we don't know
the material. You should review it with us.

LEADER   As far as I can recall, I reviewed the material
yesterday at 10 a.m. I even remember asking if anyone had
questions, and I was told everyone understood the information.

MEMBER #1   We just forgot, that's all.

LEADER   It also seems to me that everyone in the program
is given a sheet on which the defense mechanisms and their
definitions are spelled out in detail. There are examples
given.

MEMBER #1   I never got one.

MEMBER #2   Yes you did. You asked me about it the other
  day.
MEMBER #1   Show it to me.
MEMBER #2   (looks through #1's folder) Here it is.
MEMBER #1   Oh, *that's* it. I guess I didn't see it.
LEADER   Some of the members of the group are using
  defense mechanisms to justify not doing the assignments.
MEMBER #1   I am not. I didn't see the sheet. I didn't know it
  was there.
MEMBER #2   Yes you did. You're rationalizing.
MEMBER #1   Who's side are you on? You didn't know the
  stuff, either.
MEMBER #2   Yes I did. I was rationalizing, too.
LEADER   I think the entire group, including the members
  who aren't saying anything, is using defense mechanisms
  right now.
MEMBER #2   Yeah, that's on the sheet. Negativism – that's
  what it's called.
MEMBER #1   Let me get a look at that.
MEMBER #2   Why don't we go over all the defense mecha-
  nisms, so we can talk about them intelligently?
MEMBER #1   OK, that's sounds like a good idea.

Here the leader quickly uncovers the assumption of helplessness underlying the group's behavior. He then points out that
members do in fact have the information they claim not to
have. Their difficulties stem from lack of effort, not from lack of
knowledge. If some members need education in order to work
on the group's task, there are other members (such as #2) who
can provide instruction. That keeps the leader out of the teacher role.

Had the group not decided to review the defense mechanisms, the leader might well have suggested it. In either case, a
leader's objective in dealing with the helpless mode is to "get
out of the driver's seat." If he doesn't, the group simply remains
dependent, the leader's role remains preeminent, and the group
never progresses into work.

When the group does lack essential information, the members cannot provide it to one another, then the leader must teach. But once the information has been disseminated, the leader should step aside and direct the group to begin applying it.

Some leaders actually structure a group so as to make the helpless mode nearly impossible to sustain, as in the following example.

LEADER   Our task is to study defense mechanisms and how the members of the group have used them to protect drinking and to avoid treating their disease. This is your group, and my role will simply be to keep the group on-task. Other than that, the course of the group is entirely up to you.

MEMBER #1   What about if we forgot our defense mechanism sheet? Can we go get it?

(Leader doesn't answer.)

MEMBER #1   Wow. Talk about the Sphinx. Well, OK, is it OK if I leave five minutes early? My wife is coming and I want to see her briefly.

(silence)

MEMBER #2   I don't think she plans to answer.

MEMBER #1   But who leads the group?

MEMBER #2   We do. Here's the sheet. Shall we just take a few minutes to review it?

MEMBER #1   OK.

This leader has established a very clear role, one which is specifically designed to make dependency, which is characteristic of the helpless mode, extremely uncomfortable. No matter how passive the group, the leader will *not* rescue the discussion.

Activities leaders typically use to move the group out of the helpless mode include:

1. *Defining and restating the task.* Helpless groups tend to permit rambling discussion and irrelevant dialogue.

2. *Suggesting methods of discussion.* This is especially helpful with a newly formed group.
3. *Deflecting or refusing to answer questions.* Members of helpless groups are always insisting they are ignorant or uninformed or perhaps confused. Much of the time the information they need is within the group, but because members are not communicating with each other (instead depending on the leader) they aren't *aware* of their own resources.
4. *Encouraging members to instruct one another.*

DEALING WITH THE HOSTILE MODE

In the hostile mode the group takes the position that the task is unfair or excessively demanding and thus resists work actively or passively. To push the group towards work, the leader once again must identify the underlying assumption and then confront it in such a way as to reveal its invalidity. This is complicated by the group's tendency to convert any observation into personal criticism.

MEMBER #1   I am so sick of these groups. It seems like no matter what we say, we're wrong. The leader never has anything positive to say about anyone. It's just attack.

MEMBER #2   Right on. Whenever you say anything, you get told you're rationalizing or whatever.

LEADER   Pointing out defense mechanisms is the task of this group.

MEMBER #1   (angrily) I don't care! I don't plan to drink again, but being in this group makes me feel like just chucking the whole thing and going out and getting drunk!

MEMBER #2   See what you're doing? See how this group affects people?

LEADER   I think that if anyone in this group goes out and gets drunk and then blames it on the group, it would be a good example of externalizing.

MEMBER #1   That is so cold. You are a bitch, you know that?

MEMBER #2   Now, calm down. She cares about you.

LEADER   I think this group is pretty far off the track. The issue isn't whether or not the leader cares about the group. The issue is whether or not the group members care enough about sobriety to work on achieving it.

MEMBER #1   I'm trying to stay sober, and you won't let me?

MEMBER #3   But you were externalizing.

MEMBER #1   What?

MEMBER #3   You were externalizing. You were saying that you felt like getting drunk because of the group.

MEMBER #1   That's true, dammit!

MEMBER #3   Maybe. But it could also be because you've only been ten days without a drink. I mean, almost anything would make you feel like a drink at this point.

MEMBER #4   That's probably right. Maybe you're taking everything too personally. I mean, every time the leader says something you get mad, even if it's not directed towards you.

MEMBER #2   She's got a lot to be angry about, you know. This is a pretty crazy place.

MEMBER #3   It's not helping her to keep rescuing her, you know. If she talks herself into leaving, she's just going to get drunk. You're just making excuses for her.

Notice how the leader avoids any suggestion of personal confrontation with a vocal critic. Instead, she confronts the group – which includes the silent "audience" – with the fact that it is off-task. Thus, the leader sidesteps a minefield of pointless argument.

As soon as the group begins to respond – when members #3 and 4 take the initiative – the leader shuts up and gets out of the way. There is no suggestion of "I-told-you-so." The leader's goal is to get the group to work. She is not concerned with demonstrating that she was "right."

Remember that the hostile mode is an attempt to avoid the *task*. The leader merely *represents* this task. No matter how angry they may get, group members don't really "hate" their leaders. They rebel against the assumption of new and unfamiliar responsibility.

Below are some further example of leaders at work, as they push groups out of the hostile mode.

Example #1: Deflection

JOHN   I'm not talking anymore. No matter what I say, I'm wrong. I don't think this counselor knows anything about alcoholism at all. Have you ever had a drinking problem?

LEADER   Actually, the focus of these groups is supposed to be on the drinking problems of the *members*, not of the leader.

Here the leader deflects the antagonism of the critic without directly answering the critic's charges. Suppose he had informed the group that he was a recovering alcoholic? What would have been the response?

LEADER   As a matter of fact, I'm an alcoholic myself.

JOHN   Well, you ought to understand us better than you do. You've obviously forgotten what it's like to be in trouble.

It's perfectly appropriate to disclose one's own history in a work group. When in the hostile mode the group members won't respond positively. The group's critics will simply use the information against the leader.

Here's an alternative:

JOHN   What about it? Did you ever have a problem? Or did you just learn everything in school?

LEADER   I think the group needs to get something clear. Alcoholism is a disease. Most diseases are treated by people who do *not* have the disease. When you have cancer, you don't look for a doctor who *also* has cancer. You look for a doctor who knows how to *treat* cancer. If you want to share experiences with other people who have your disease, you go to a group, like a cancer support group, or AA. But if you want to work on specific problems that affect the treatment of your disease, you go to a task-oriented group like this one. Our purpose here is set forth very clearly in the task, which, in case you've forgotten, is. . . .

This leader has deflected the focus back to the disease and to the specific goals of the group. This is helpful because it is the disease, rather than the group, that threatens the lives of the members. Contrary to popular belief, treatment does *not* kill people. Alcoholism does.

Example #2: Retreat

MARK   I hate groups. I hate having to explain everything I do or say. I hate being told I am using defense mechanisms. I mean, they tell you to talk, and then they criticize everything you say.

LEADER   Suppose I shut up completely? Would the group agree to keep itself on task?

LISA   Sure we would.

LEADER   All right then. I won't say anything as long as you are on task.

(Brief silence follows.)

FRANK   Does anybody know when dinner is?

LISA   That's off-task, Frank.

This is a dandy little manipulation. By giving in to the group's resistance, the leader gets members to agree to work, at least to the point of keeping their own boundaries.

Example #3: Confrontation

JEAN   (to leader) You know, sometimes I get the feeling that you really don't care for us at all. You seem so unfeeling.

JOYCE   We've all discussed that. We think you really ought to unbend a little. You make us uncomfortable.

LEADER   So my behavior is the reason people won't talk in group, is it?

HENRY   (angrily) Yes it is! The last time you were here, you
     were so negative I had to leave!
LEADER   Am I to believe a member of this group left the
     program and got drunk just because of me?
HENRY   That's absolutely right!
LEADER   And did you get sick?
HENRY   You know I did! You saw me in detox!
LEADER   That's funny. *I* didn't get sick at all.

In this exchange the leader goes right after the group's defenses. He shows that Henry used the leader as an excuse to
drink and, in fact, suffered because of his own rationalization.
Just as the leader can't get sick when a member drinks, he
cannot take responsibility for the success or failure of the members in treatment.

   This group expects the leader to provide warmth, caring,
and support—which are provided more effectively by family,
friends, and AA. Treatment, on the other hand, can give a
person *self-knowledge*, which, as we all know, sometimes comes
painfully.

Passive hostility may be a bit more difficult to handle than
the active hostility seen in previous examples. It will be dis-
guised as something other than hostility.

LEADER   I noticed that three people were late to group.
     Does this have anything to do with how mad people got in
     yesterday's session?
(silence)
LEADER   Seems as though the group members have gotten
     together and decided not to talk today.
(more silence)
LEADER   Also, I see that Joan is knitting, and John is
     reading *Time* magazine, and Bob is asleep. Doesn't look
     promising.
JOAN   Maybe we just don't have anything to talk about
     today.
JOHN   Yeah, silence doesn't always mean the group is mad.

RUTH   Why don't you talk? We'll listen for a while. Maybe we'll learn something for a change.

JOHN   If we look mad, that means that you have a problem, because I'm not mad, and I don't think anybody else is, either. That's just *your* obsession. Everybody always has to be mad about something.

RUTH   We just don't have anything to say. We're all talked out.

LEADER   If the group is talked out, why don't people just leave?

RUTH   What do you mean? We can't leave. We're in the program, and the group is mandatory.

LEADER   Why not leave the program? Why stay when you have nothing to say?

JOHN   I can't leave. I've got a court case pending.

RUTH   I promised my kids I would stay.

PETE   I'll get thrown out of the house.

MARY   My doctor says I can't go home, I'm still too sick.

LEADER   Sounds like there are plenty of reasons to be in treatment for alcoholism. Therefore, there should be plenty to talk about. That is, unless you want to discuss it *next* time you're in treatment.

This is an example of deflection combined with confrontation. When the leader encounters passive hostility, he ignores the group's contention that members are "talked out" and instead redirects attention to the problems that brought members to treatment in the first place. Since all treatment is motivated by pain and problems associated with drinking or drug use, this helps to "remotivate" the group.

DEALING WITH THE HOPEFUL EXPECTATION MODE

The hopeful expectation mode usually reveals itself through the formation of pairs of members. These pairs assume some leadership functions, usually by allowing the group to remain dependent, and thereby achieve some temporary improvement in morale.

Leaders frequently play into the hopeful expectation mode. Discouraged by a balky group, they accept compromises which provide the form of work without the changes that should result. Since the leader is such an important part of this mode, intervention from the Leader is almost always required to move out of it.

LEADER   I've been thinking about something the past few weeks. I don't see much change going on in this group. We talk about a lot of problems, but we don't accomplish much.

DENISE   I don't know what you mean. We like the group. It's much better now than a few months ago. Then all we did was argue. Now we talk and share our feelings, and I feel better.

RICK   Yeah, I think the group has really come together. I know most people don't talk much, but they're just shy, and I think maybe we'll get them out of their shells in the future.

LEADER   It still seems to me that the group has fallen into a pattern of talking about things, but not changing behavior.

DENISE   That's not true. We change things.

LEADER   Last week we spent most of our session on Denise's problem with her husband, but then ten minutes ago she tells the group she didn't get around to confronting him during the week.

LEADER   (continuing) And two weeks ago, the group spent the whole session on Rick's problems, and everyone made a lot of suggestions, and yet we found out that Rick didn't actually put any of those suggestions to work.

RICK   I'm afraid I have to object to that. I feel we've all made a lot of progress, and you're just acting like we've been wasting time. I don't think that shows a very high opinion of the group on your part.

(Leader doesn't answer.)

DENISE   You can't expect us to change overnight. I know I don't always follow through on things. But it's hard.

(more silence)

RICK   Well, what about some of the rest of you? You come to
this group, but you never talk. Why don't you do your
share? What do you think? Does anything happen in this
group, or not?

JEAN   I don't think a lot happens, to be honest. We mainly
just listen to you.

RICK   Well, that's *your* problem. You *could* talk if you
wanted to. I just don't enjoy sitting here silently for a
whole hour, which is what would happen if we left it up to
you.

LEADER   I wonder if that's true. I wonder if perhaps the
group shouldn't try something different.

DENISE   I feel sorry for Rick. He's tried to keep this group
going, without a lot of help, and nobody seems to appreciate him.

(Group remains silent.)

DENISE   I wouldn't blame him if he never spoke again, with
all the grief he's getting for it.

LEADER   Perhaps some of the other members of the group
have an opinion.

(silence)

RICK   See? Nothing. This is a lively group. We ought to hold
our meetings at the city morgue.

JEAN   Well, one of the reasons I don't talk is because the
group is always discussing something that has nothing to
do with me.

DENISE   I don't know how you can say that.

RICK   I think you're just in denial. You think you're better
than the rest of us.

JEAN   (angrily) No, I don't. I think that you think you're
better than the others in this group. That's why you never
listen to any of the suggestions we give you.

RICK   That's absurd.

JEAN   No, it isn't. You soak up all this attention, and then
you don't change anything. And the leader finally called
your attention to it, and you're all of a sudden mad at
everybody.

RICK   I am *not* angry. You are projecting your feelings onto
me.

DENISE   I think we've heard enough of this. Attacking Rick
isn't going to help anything.

JEAN   And you're always rescuing him. The two of you run
your own group, and we sit here like your audience.

RICK   I think you shouldn't speak for the whole group.
James, do you feel that way about Denise and myself?

JAMES   Well . . . no, I don't feel that way, I guess.

RICK   (to Jean) See? Your support wasn't as broad as you
thought.

JEAN   James, you told me after the group last week that
you were going to drop out because the group was completely irrelevant to you, and you were bored to tears.

JAMES   Well . . . uh, I . . . well, I meant. . . .

JEAN   And I give Sally a ride, and half the time I have to
spend time talking her into coming to the group, because
she says the two of you won't let anyone get a word in
edgewise. So maybe it's *you* who don't know what's going
on.

LEADER   Looks like the group has a problem. Perhaps we
should spend the rest of this session taking a look at the
group, rather than at outside problems.

(brief silence)

RICK   I don't know. Maybe I should just drop out, if nobody
wants me here.

JEAN   That's not what we said. And you know it. Don't feel
sorry for yourself.

Once again, the leader challenges the *underlying assumptions* of the hopeful expectation mode, rather than the individual members who perpetuate it. In this case, the assumption is
that the group is functioning well, despite the fact that only
two members speak and they dominate discussion without
making productive changes.

A challenging leader will find considerable dependency and
hostility underneath the hopeful expectation mode. Thus, a
group pushed out of this mode often regresses into helplessness

or tries to pick a fight with the leader. The group is in fact quite nonfunctional, having dedicated itself to providing only the *illusion* of work.

MAINTAINING WORK

In addition to promoting work, the leader may do any number of things to support the work mode once it appears. Essentially, the leader sets himself the task of providing the group with functions not currently provided by members. Thus, in the work mode, the leader may self-disclose relevant information from his own experience, taking the role of a working member, or perhaps serve as a gatekeeper at the group's boundaries. The nature of this mode is that roles are flexible, and the group essentially governs itself.

Typical maintenance functions include:

- *Assisting others in assuming leadership:* When a member begins to flounder in his role of assumed leadership, the leader can show him how to handle various problems.
- *Sharing:* Usually of personal experience that contributes to the Work of the group at that time.
- *Harmonizing:* Agreeing with, complimenting, or joining along with the work of the group at that point in time.
- *Reconciling differences:* If conflicts emerge within the group, the leader can help reconcile them.
- *Discipline:* When the group requires external authority, the leader can provide this. The leader may be called upon to handle interruptions from outside or distracting behavior by a sick or crazy member.
- *Gatekeeping:* Leaders start and end the group. This avoids the *"bomb syndrome"* (members bringing up problems two minutes before the session ends, thus necessitating an extension of the group) and *lateness.*

Even in the work mode, individual members will try to push the group away from work. Typical disruption tactics include:

- *Aggressing:* Attacking the leader or an active member in order to disrupt work. Rule #1: Don't defend yourself or answer specific accusations. The leader has nothing to prove to the group, and the members aren't there to evaluate the leader's skills. Simply direct the group members to return to the task. If they don't, point out to them that no work is being done, and no progress can result. Remind the group members that only they can produce the results they say they want. Or investigate with them exactly why they are so uncomfortable with the task.
- *Blocking:* Refusing to participate or interfering with discussion. This is simply a passive form of the previous tactic. Use the same approach: Avoid interaction with individual members and address all comments about the disruptive behavior and its probable meaning to the group. Remind the group members that they are *permitting* the behavior to continue, indicating a desire to avoid work.
- *Joking:* Disrupting a discussion with jokes – especially of dubious taste – is a common avoidance. When this happens, immediately remind the group of the task. Restate it if necessary.
- *Dominating discussion:* Extreme willingness to participate can also disrupt work by interfering with anyone else's ability to comment. Point out to the group that one member is doing all the talking, which probably isn't going to help the rest of them stay sober.
- *Help-seeking:* Attempting to focus attention exclusively on oneself. Helpless or hopeful expectation groups often feature a "problem child" who is always good for a discussion topic when nobody wants to work. Inform the group members that they're not in the audience of *The Oprah Winfrey Show* and that they all have problems that need work.
- *Special interest pleas:* Asking for dispensations to leave early, avoid participation, etc., are a way of exempting oneself from work. Remind the group of the boundaries and their purpose, and hold them to those boundaries. A rough guideline: If you're well enough to be in the group, you're well enough to participate.

CHAPTER 8

ALCOHOLICS ANONYMOUS AS A WORKING GROUP

ALCOHOLICS ANONYMOUS might be considered the most effective form of group therapy yet developed. We can't think of anything that surpasses it. What has made AA so beneficial where other modalities have failed? How has an organization dedicated to *nonprofessionalism* outperformed sophisticated treatment?

To understand the forces behind AA's success, we must study the organization at its most basic level: the AA meeting. It is here that AA interacts with the "suffering alcoholic" mentioned in AA literature. And on this plane, AA functions much like any good, healthy "small group." AA itself, we believe, is really a loose confederation of thousands upon thousands of such groups, each possessing many of the characteristics, good and bad, that we have discussed in this book.

In the following pages we examine AA in the terms of group process. As we go, we might expect to find that AA meetings, quite without the "benefit" of professional guidance, have managed to incorporate many of the features of work groups – and, in fact, are of a quality to be *envied* by many clinicians. This is a good lesson in humility for those of us who do this for a living. The founders of AA, we imagine, would appreciate that.

Just as AA meetings vary in size and composition, they also

vary in quality. As one longtime member advised us, "If you've never been to a bad AA meeting, you just haven't been to enough meetings." Nevertheless, AA manages to appeal to those alcoholics just emerging from detox as well as those who haven't touched a drop in 20 years. That is a broad range of appeal, indeed.

AA meetings, like any small groups, tend to go through a period of instability during their first year of existence. Some die, while others flourish. When a group survives its growing pains, it often becomes a paragon of stability. Many AA groups are as stable as the churches or hospitals which house them.

Meetings are amazingly easy to start. All you need, the saying goes, is two drunks and a coffeepot.

Suppose Alfred, a longtime AA member, is transferred to an area where the closest meeting is 30 miles away. After a few months of commuting, he decides that it would be a good idea to start a new group closer to home. He rents a room in the local church, heats up a pot of coffee, and spreads the word via the AA grapevine that he'll be at St. Edna's at 8 P.M. on Tuesdays. If anybody is in the neighborhood, drop in and you can have an AA meeting.

At first, one or two people show up. But after six months or so, new people transfer into the area and the group experiences an influx of new members. By its second year of existence, the meeting numbers 30 regular attendees.

Then Alfred gets transferred to yet another remote area. The meeting he started continues after he leaves. And since he still has his coffeepot, he may just start another meeting in his new home.

Each group follows broad general guidelines set forth by AA's headquarters in New York and attempts to govern itself according to the Twelve Traditions, which are designed to nurture and protect both the organization as a whole and the member groups. But in addition, each group establishes its own practices, traditions, and boundaries, so that every AA group is as unique as the alcoholics who attend it.

Let's look at the dynamics and structure of AA, much as we examined the professional groups in preceding chapters.

BONDING

AA groups bond positively around the idea that the *group itself* is the key to recovery for the members. Recall that every AA member has tried—and failed—at sobriety on his or her own. AA, then, is something of a "court of last resort." What will make the difference for the alcoholic, enabling him to succeed where past efforts have met with failure? Most AA's would probably cite three factors: the Higher Power, the Twelve Step program, and the AA group itself.

As tradition one states: "Our common welfare should come first; personal recovery depends on AA unity." Individual ambition—of which alcoholics have plenty—is *devalued* in relation to the importance of the group. As the group matures, it is seen as nurturing and protecting the sobriety of its members. This is in stark contrast to many psychotherapy groups, where individual needs, desires, and ambitions are emphasized and encouraged. AA, on the other hand, takes extreme care that *no individual*, no matter how talented, achieves a position of dominance or special privilege within the group.

To understand the thinking behind this, compare it with the experience of a drug treatment program which achieved some notoriety in years past. This program, like AA, had been founded by a charismatic man under whose leadership a group of addicts bonded together in an effort to rebuild their lives. The leader and his followers moved into a commune and began working small miracles among the "incorrigibles" who joined them. They operated their own businesses, married and raised families. Though some of the trappings of democracy were preserved, everyone acknowledged that important decisions were the province of the leader. This, they believed, was as it should be. It was the leader's vision that had brought them success in the past.

After a number of years, the leader decided that it would be a good idea for his community to try again to use alcohol safely. Although this had been impossible for them in the years before they came together, they thought the intervening years of growth and maturity would prevent a reoccurrence of problems. The experiment was a dismal failure. The leader himself, back on alcohol, began to deteriorate. His decisions became capricious. Despite this, those around him were supportive, even protective. They continued to carry out his wishes, even if dangerous. Finally, the leader violated the laws of the land, and the organization (and all its troubles) was paraded through court. Naturally, both the leader and the organization lost enormous prestige.

AA's own beginnings featured a certain amount of dependence upon charismatic, visionary leaders such as Bill Wilson and Dr. Bob Smith. It isn't hard to imagine AA taking a course similar to that of the organization in our example. But as AA grew, it made a crucial decision: to abandon this sort of dependence in favor of awkward self-determination. Bill Wilson continued as a revered figure, but had he "gone round the bend," AA would not have gone with him.

CLIMATE

The background climate of an AA meeting—those attitudes the members bring *with* them—is best described in the first step: "Admitted we were powerless over alcohol—that our lives had become unmanageable." AA members constantly remind one another of this background through the "drunkalogue": each member's tale of chaos as his disease dominated his life.

This contributes to a foreground climate of mutual reliance on one another. AA members alternately support and confront each other. They "deflate" pretensions and ambitions they believe might threaten sobriety. Credit for recovery is invariably given to AA or the Higher Power, rather than to the individual.

VALUES

AA groups value abstinence, continued attendance, fellowship, and personal growth for their members. But for the *group itself*, one value outstrips all others: *autonomy*.

AA groups strive to maintain their independence from out-

side influence, from centralized authority within AA, and from
the ambitions of their own members.
Let's review a few of AA's Twelve Traditions.

* Tradition Two: "For our group purpose, there is but one ultimate authority – a loving God as He may express Himself in
  our group conscience. Our leaders are but trusted servants;
  they do not govern."
* Tradition Four: "Each group should be autonomous except in
  matters affecting other groups or AA as a whole."
* Tradition Six: "An AA group ought never to endorse, finance,
  or lend the AA name to any related facility or outside enter-
  prise. . . ."
* Tradition Seven: "Every AA group ought to be fully self-
  supporting, declining outside contributions."
* Tradition Eight: "Alcoholics Anonymous should remain forever nonprofessional."
* Tradition Nine: "AA, as such, ought never to be organized."
* Tradition Ten: "Alcoholics Anonymous has no opinion on outside issues. . . ."
* Tradition Eleven: "We need always maintain personal anonymity at the level of press, radio, and films."

Clearly, the founders believed that AA could be abused, and
therefore deserved special protection.

Abuse can come from outside the group or from within it.
The only real safeguard for the group – upon which the personal recovery of members *depends* – lies in the abandonment of an
easy and comfortable dependence, avoidance of the trappings
of "success," and assumption of full responsibility for choosing
and controlling its own destiny.

As one member put it, "that's quite a responsibility to give a
bunch of former drunks – and it's exactly what we need."

To avoid abuse of authority within the group, AA meetings
constantly rotate leadership. Tradition nine clarifies this: "True
leaders in AA are but experienced and trusted servants. They
derive no real authority from their titles. . . . Universal respect
is the key to their usefulness."

STRUCTURE

In the absence of externally designated leaders, roles and status are determined entirely by the group. There is only one "outside" authority recognized in the traditions: " . . . a loving God, as He may express Himself in our group conscience." A group conscience is a vote by the membership on an issue, policy, or procedure important to them. But unlike political elections, which are often decided by prejudice and personal ambition, the group conscience places the membership in the position of having to decide what is "right," *according to the principles of AA.* In other words, it's a "moral" election. AA assumes that where individuals might waver in their commitment to AA's principles, the group as a whole will not.

AA meetings vary greatly in format. At some meetings, one or two speakers relate their experience, lecture-style; at others, a topic is presented for discussion. Some meetings are restricted to alcoholics only, while others are open. And numerous "specialty meetings" cater to most subgroups in society. Functions within the meeting – secretary, program chairman, etc. – are assigned on a rotating basis.

AA goes to considerable lengths to place responsibility for participation on the alcoholic himself. One slogan reminds members that "AA is for those who *want* it, not for those who *need* it." Tradition three reminds that "the only requirement for membership is a desire to stop drinking" – and who can determine that but the drinker himself? Still another slogan insists that AA "carries the message, but not the alcoholic": don't expect loans or free room and board along with the Twelve Steps.

AA's groups must be classified as broadly *task-oriented.* Though discussion may wander, it is always brought back to the "experience, strength, and hope" which recovery brought to each AA member. And in joining AA, the alcoholic takes upon himself joint responsibility for AA's "primary purpose": "to carry the message to the alcoholic who still suffers" (tradition five). This larger task converts each member into an instructor in the art of recovering from alcoholism and turns AA itself into a "school for sobriety."

TRADITIONS

There are, of course, the formal Twelve Traditions (from which we've quoted liberally), as well as numerous informal traditions reflecting the customs of individual groups. For example, many meetings recite the Lord's Prayer at meeting's conclusion. The Twelve Traditions neither endorse nor discourage this.

In the absence of more formal structure, traditions become all-important. Though often unwritten and with their origins forgotten by many AA members, traditions survive generations of transition in membership. Such traditions have truly become "the way we do things in this group."

MENTALITY

The group is primary, and without the group the members might not recover. Thus, preservation of the group and its principles becomes paramount. Individual needs, while important, are secondary.

CULTURE

When conflicts emerge within a group — and they most certainly do — they are resolved by the group conscience, or by trial and error, or by the formation of a new meeting. The culture of AA is best expressed by tradition twelve: "Anonymity is the spiritual foundation of all our traditions, forever reminding us to place principles before personalities." Thus anonymity is revealed as more than a device for preserving confidentiality. It is an integral part of the process of "ego deflation" which underlies AA's approach. Perhaps this anonymity has permitted AA to survive — better than other, less "unusual" organizations — the ambitions and inconsistencies of its own membership.

AA teaches us a lesson which professional therapists have been slow to learn: that the interaction of the group—positive, task-oriented, and homogeneous—is crucial to recovery. *Not*, we must conclude, professional guidance or therapeutic insight. It seems to us that much professional training is oriented towards teaching therapists to treat alcoholics, when instead we should concentrate on showing therapists how to let alcoholics treat one another.

CHAPTER 9

TOWARDS GROUPS THAT WORK

IN KEEPING WITH our emphasis on practical application, we conclude with an illustration of what it is like to work in a program that uses task-oriented groups. Here are some excerpts from a supervisory session in a treatment center which has made the decision to switch from *issue-oriented* to *task-oriented* groups. While it isn't a group, it does provide an opportunity for leaders to review their just completed sessions with a supervisor, Frank. Jeff, Steve, Beverly, and Susan are new trainees in a group leadership program.

FRANK   OK, why don't we start by going over what happened in each group? Keep it brief—just the highlights and any particular problems you may have had. We'll go into more depth later. Our purpose is to review process while the group is fresh in our minds. Jeff, why don't you begin?

JEFF   I don't think you want to start with me. My group was a complete bust.

FRANK   What happened?

JEFF   Well, to begin with, I couldn't get them to do anything. I gave them a task, like you said, but they just sat there. They seemed to have no idea what to do with it.

FRANK   How long before they said anything?

JEFF   It seemed like forever. I would have sworn 15 or 20 minutes had passed before they said anything at all. But when I checked my watch, it was only three or four minutes.

FRANK   Then what happened?

JEFF   They started talking about something that was
          completely unrelated to the task. Like they never even
          heard me say it. So I tried to bring them back, and that
          made it worse. Finally, one of them explained that the
          group really didn't understand what was expected of them.

FRANK   How did you respond?

JEFF   I told them that this was a different type of group,
          and that we were supposed to talk about a task instead of
          whatever anyone wanted to bring up. The one fellow who'd
          spoken up earlier said that was impossible because he
          couldn't understand the task. So he didn't see how he could
          be expected to discuss it.

FRANK   And you did what?

JEFF   I did my best to explain it, naturally. I told him the
          purpose of the group was to help the members identify the
          symptoms of alcoholism or drug dependency in their
          experience, so they could understand they had a disease. It
          turned out he wasn't even sure what those symptoms were,
          so we spent most of the rest of the session going over them.
          I know that's a lot of time and I'm not supposed to be that
          active, but I think there were a lot of people in the group
          who weren't clear and I think I helped everybody quite a
          bit.

FRANK   Maybe. Let me ask, how do you know that all the
          group members were getting some benefit from what you
          were doing?

JEFF   Well, they looked interested. Maybe they didn't say
          much, although they weren't totally silent, either. They did
          make comments and ask questions . . . but they seemed
          more involved than at the beginning of the session.

FRANK   Did they make use of the information you gave
          them? After all this teaching, did they then become more
          active in doing the task?

JEFF   No, not really. To be honest, there wasn't a whole lot
          of time left. But I think they'll be a lot better prepared for
          the next session.

FRANK   Possibly. But my question is: How do you know?

Since they didn't make any particular use of the information, how can you be sure that the session was of any value?

JEFF   Just a gut feeling, I guess. It seemed like they hadn't heard the information before, so getting it explained had to be of some value. Plus several of them told me after the session that they felt they'd learned a lot. I don't see how we can expect them to use information that we hadn't given them. It isn't fair.

FRANK   Had they been in that particular group before?

JEFF   Most of them. There was one newcomer, but I don't remember him saying anything. The fellow who was speaking – the one I spent most of the time with – he's leaving the program this week. So it's good I spent the time with him. I'd hate to think he's going to go home with no more information than he had at the start of the session.

FRANK   Doesn't that make you suspicious?

JEFF   Of what?

FRANK   Of a guy who has been in a treatment program for 30 days and still doesn't understand the symptoms of addiction. There's no way he could have gotten past the first *week* without being taught this information. Did he appear to have some kind of learning disability?

JEFF   Not at all. He's an engineer. He's very articulate.

FRANK   Got a terrible memory? Alzheimer's, perhaps?

JEFF   You're being sarcastic. He's perfectly capable of learning whatever he sets his mind to.

FRANK   Well then, it seems to me we have two choices. Either this fellow has gotten absolutely nothing out of his stay here – in which case your explanation of the task was probably a waste of time – or you had a group that was resisting work.

BEVERLY   It's the helpless mode. The group assumes they don't have the information to work on the task. They try to get you to do it for them. That turns the group into a lecture, and they get off the hook. I got the same thing last week from my group.

JEFF   (looks at Frank) Is that right?

FRANK   Sounds logical to me. Here's why: You've only got
one newcomer. Everyone else has already been exposed to
this information and to this task. The one member who
insists he doesn't understand the task is a very bright
individual scheduled to graduate in a couple of days. Yet
out of the blue, they're stricken with a sudden attack of
ignorance, and you wind up teaching basic information as
though they just arrived yesterday.

JEFF   But they seemed to like it.

FRANK   I imagine it's fun. After all, you do all the work.

JEFF   Well, I still think some people got a lot out of the
group.

FRANK   I'm sure they learned something. But did they learn
how to work as a group? I don't think so. But here's the
acid test: Give them the same task tomorrow, and see if
they have similar problems. In other words, see if they try
to put you back in the teaching position.

JEFF   I still don't get it. You're saying that even though the
member I worked with got a lot out of the session, the
group was a total failure?

FRANK   Stop thinking of it in terms of success and failure.
And stop thinking about the effect on the life of an individual member. Remember, you're a *group* leader; that means
your attention should be focused on the group. Look at
your session in terms of *work* and *nonwork*, which are
modes that appear in groups. For example, if a group sits
silently while a leader works with one member, you have to
assume the members think this is the way group is supposed to work. You think you're teaching one member
about something important, but at the same time you're
teaching the rest of the group to sit there and watch you
work. I don't know how to make that any simpler. Try this:
You thought you were teaching them about the task. What
they learned was that it's your job to teach them, and their
job to do nothing.

JEFF   I think I'm beginning to understand. But why do the
others look interested?

FRANK   You're probably an entertaining teacher. But that

doesn't mean they were applying the information to themselves.

JEFF   What else could I have done?

FRANK   You could have challenged the group to do the
teaching. Put the members who did have the information in
the position of transmitting it to others. Point out that if
the newcomer or anyone else in the group needed help, one
or more of them were perfectly capable of providing it. And
in fact, that's why they're in a group instead of a classroom.
Remember, what's appropriate to the lecture hall isn't
appropriate to the group session. They're in class to learn;
they're in group to *make use of* what they learned.

JEFF   Then I wasn't giving the group credit for what
they've already absorbed. I joined in their belief that they
couldn't do the task.

FRANK   I think that's a good summary. If you keep reminding yourself why we have group therapy, you'll never lose
sight of that.

Note how Frank constantly emphasizes the importance of
assessing the group rather than the individual. That's probably
the single most difficult change for someone accustomed to the
therapist role. Jeff's natural inclination—reinforced perhaps by
his previous training—is to focus on one or two participants
and to employ the techniques of one-to-one psychotherapy.
Frank points out that this actually *negates* the value of being
in a group.

Let's go back to the session:

FRANK   Bev, what about your group?

BEVERLY   Mine was the opposite of Jeff's. They weren't
helpless, but it still went very badly, for a different reason.
I think I know what I did wrong. I should have . . .

FRANK   Save the verdict for later. Just tell us what happened in the session.

BEVERLY   OK. This was an outpatient group, remember.
But they're pretty new in treatment. I think there's one
fellow who's been to more than five meetings; the others are

relatively new. And last week they were horribly dependent,
like Jeff's group. Wouldn't cooperate at all. So this time, I
let them stew a little at the start. And then, believe it or
not, it looked like they were actually trying to work. They
struggled some, but they got hold of the list of symptoms
and began going over them with the newer members. I was
really surprised how much information they had . . . you'd
never have known it from last week's session. They seemed
to be getting somewhere, until this one member – Jake, I
think you know him – got disruptive. I tried to intervene,
but I wasn't sure what I was supposed to do, and I need to
review. . . .

FRANK   Once again, let's just describe what happened. We'll
evaluate it later.

BEVERLY   Well, they were talking about alcoholic blackouts.
They were going around the group and asking each member
if he'd experienced a blackout, and if so to relate the
experience to the group. About halfway through, Jake gets
mad at Bill for dominating the discussion. He told Bill that
he was acting like a counselor and he didn't think Bill was
any better qualified to be a therapist than he was. Bill tried
to answer, but Jake just ignored him and went on this
tirade about how he already knew he had a drinking problem, that's why he was in this group, but he wasn't going to
apply the label *alcoholic* to himself, because he wasn't one.
No matter what we said, he knew perfectly well he never
would be. And he wasn't going to let the group bully him
into saying it.

FRANK   The group's response?

BEVERLY   Well, I intervened at that point. I pointed out
that the task was to identify symptoms, not to pin the
label "alcoholic" on people.

FRANK   And?

BEVERLY   He ignored it. Actually, it seemed to make him
even angrier. He asked me for my qualifications. I explained I was trained as a therapist. He said that was why
I couldn't understand an uneducated person like him. So I
went on to explain that I was also a recovering alcoholic,

and in fact I'd gone through a program five years ago, so I knew how he was feeling. That didn't seem to help at all, which surprised me. He accused me of being "holier than thou" and said I had to justify my salary by seeing everyone as an alcoholic. I felt like braining him. What should I have done? I felt so helpless.

FRANK   Before we get to that . . . what was the rest of the group doing during this exchange?

BEVERLY   Nothing, I guess. Listening. Bill tried to interrupt but Jake just rolled on. So he shut up, too. Finally, Jake was so angry I got a little worried, and suggested he go see the nurse and have his blood pressure checked, and excused him from the rest of the session. I probably shouldn't have done that, but I was getting worried about him. I thought he might have a stroke or something. You should have seen his face . . .

FRANK   How much time remained after Jake left? And what did the group do with it?

BEVERLY   Maybe 15 minutes. They talked about Jake, of course. Louise was upset, and we talked about how Jake reminded her of her father, and how angry he would get when he'd been drinking. There's a real ACOA issue there, I think. I pointed that out, and she and I spent a few minutes talking about an incident from when she was a teenager. And I spent some time letting people ventilate, reassuring them that it was all right to get angry in group . . . that nobody was going to die or anything.

FRANK   If you really believe that, then why did you ask Jake to leave? Wasn't it because you were afraid he'd drop dead?

BEVERLY   I see what you mean . . . well, I guess I meant that *they* wouldn't die because Jake got angry.

FRANK   So what did the group accomplish?

BEVERLY   Well, they started off well. I think maybe Jake should have been held back another week – maybe he still needed some detoxifying. Obviously, he wasn't ready for the group. I think maybe he ought not to be there for a while.

FRANK   Why not?

BEVERLY   He's too angry, and that upsets everyone. It
interferes with the work, as you always say. I don't think
people can recover with somebody like Jake in the session.

FRANK   Jeff, Bev gave you an analysis of your group. What
mode do you see in hers?

JEFF   Hostile, obviously. Jake was the ringleader, but the
group permitted him to roam on. Bill tried to interrupt, but
they didn't support him, so that means he was expressing
their feelings.

BEVERLY   But they didn't seem angry to me. Only Jake.
And I know Bill was trying to work.

FRANK   The hostile mode is a form of resistance, not an
expression of feeling. It means the group actively opposes
the task and the leader. They expressed that by permitting
Jake to take up more than half the session, attacking your
qualifications, the motivation of another member who was
attempting to work, and the task itself. They didn't allow
Bill to work, either. They left you dangling in the wind, and
when Jake left, they made no attempt to get to the task.
Even though he was no longer present, he was still a good
excuse for avoiding work.

BEVERLY   You mean they did all this on purpose?

FRANK   Not at all. I think you're confusing meaning with
intent. They're not really angry with you, Bev; they don't
even know you. They weren't trying to hurt your feelings.
Their goal was simply to avoid work and the anxiety it
brings . . . to get you to stop talking about something that
threatens them.

Think of it this way: First they bond around the idea that
the task is unfair. Everything else they do follows from
that assumption. They have to allow Jake to rant and rave
and can't make any attempt to control him, because to do
so would mean they thought the task was fair. They had to
put you in the position of confronting Jake – and thus
bearing the brunt of his anger – because to prevent that
would have challenged their assumption that the task was
unfair.

BEVERLY   But Jake was so angry. Do you really think they
could have stopped him?

FRANK   My guess is they could have stopped him whenever
they wanted. Suppose two or three of the stronger members
told Jake he was off task, that his anger was unjustified,
and that he was interfering with treatment. Suppose they
pointed out his denial and implied that was what got him
in this mess in the first place. Do you really think he was
prepared to sustain his tantrum against concerted pressure
from his peers?

BEVERLY   You know, now that you mention it, it's almost as
though they started to work, then got scared and bolted
like frightened horses.

FRANK   Not a bad analogy. In response, you might have
reminded them that they were off task, and it was their
responsibility to get back on task – including dealing with
Jake. Put the burden on the group.

BEVERLY   So I shouldn't have intervened.

FRANK   No . . . you should have intervened, but in a different way. You made the same choice Jeff did: You acted in
response to the individual instead of the group. When you
do that, your role switches from group leader to individual
therapist. And what's the impact on the group? So you
shouldn't be surprised that after Jake left, they turned to
you for solace and support. In their eyes, that's what you're
there to provide. I'd give you the same advice I gave Jeff:
Speak to the group rather than the individual. When Jake
starts to get angry, don't respond directly to him. Instead,
point out to the group members that they're letting the
session stray from the task. Ask the group to bring it back.
Tell them it's their group and their responsibility.

BEVERLY   Then what really happened is this: they went
from helplessness to work, with Bill taking the lead. They
switched to active hostility, with Jake as their spokesman.
After he left, they fell back into helpless mode – with me, I
suppose, as the kindly therapist. And very little of this had
anything to do with the task.

FRANK   That's what it sounds like to me. When a group is working, leadership changes with ability – whoever is best prepared for a given task. When a group is in the hostile mode, the member most willing to express anger becomes the spokesman. When they return to helplessness, the designated leader becomes the natural focus of their desire to depend on someone.

BEVERLY   I get it.

FRANK   Whenever you take the responsibility off the shoulders of the group, you eliminate the chance for work.

In one respect, Beverly's error was the same as Jeff's: She got "hooked" into an exchange with one member. Instead of teaching, however, she found herself defending the task against a hostile challenger, to the point of eventually tossing him out of the group. And like Jeff, she did not give the group credit for being able to solve its own problems – a position which usually results in attempts by the leader to *rescue* the session, which in turn thrusts the group back into the helpless mode.

(Later in the discussion:

STEVE   Well, I guess I'm next. I lucked out. My group worked from beginning to end. They talked without prompting, had a lot to say, and it seemed that everybody was clear about how helpful the group was.

FRANK   What did they talk about?

STEVE   Well, this is an inpatient group, remember. There was one member who left the program against medical advice last night. Apparently he'd been using cocaine in the program, and when they asked him for a urine sample, he ran. Before they got a chance to toss him out, I guess.

The funny part is that I'm sure most of the members knew about the drug use, but didn't say anything. Because they said they felt it wasn't their place. But when he did leave, it was pretty clear they were relieved. I think one or two of them were angry with him for betraying their trust – Bernice in particular, this older woman, said she felt he had failed to meet the minimum expectations and ought not to be readmitted even if he agrees to submit to urine screens. I explained to her that even though he lied to us, he also lied to himself – that he'd probably convinced himself that he was doing OK despite the slips he was having. I think that perspective was valuable to her. There was a great deal of participation, and I think that group will be stronger for the experience.

FRANK   Sounds terrific. One question: how many people were in the group?

STEVE   (thinks for a moment) Nine.

FRANK   How many talked during the session?

STEVE   All of them.

FRANK   They all had more to say than just a brief comment?

STEVE   Well, some of them didn't say much. But that's probably just the way they are. Bernice talked a lot, which is typical, and of course Howard was very active. He's a lawyer, and I suspect he can't tolerate silence.

FRANK   I see. Just as an experiment, let's go through the group one by one and see how many talked, and what they had to say.

STEVE   Well, there was Rory. I remember he talked about . . . no, that was Howard. I guess Rory didn't say anything . . . he seemed interested, though.

FRANK   How about Joanne? Or Ruth?

STEVE   Ruth was very quiet. But Joanne was about to jump out of her skin. Howard confessed to the group that he'd been aware that Ben, the guy who got thrown out, was using coke. I got the distinct impression that she'd known too. I think she was afraid Howard was going to say that she'd hidden it from the staff.

FRANK   She said that?

STEVE   No, I inferred it from her behavior.

FRANK   Which behavior?

STEVE   I don't know . . . nothing in particular. You know how sometimes you just sense things. I got the distinct impression something was bothering her. From a gesture or something.

FRANK   What gesture? Combing her hair? Blowing her nose?

STEVE   OK, OK. I know I'm being vague. It was the way she sat on the edge of her seat, hanging on each word. Very tense.

FRANK   So she seemed tense when Howard was talking about Ben, and you assumed that was because she'd known about Ben using drugs and that Howard would reveal this to the group.

STEVE   I think so. I kept my eye on her the entire group.

FRANK   Okay. Now: what was *the rest of the group* doing while you were talking with Howard and keeping an eye on Joanne?

STEVE   Listening. Participating.

FRANK   Tell us how. Describe their participation.

STEVE   Well . . . I remember Lois saying she thought it was terrible. And there was a new guy named Mark . . . I think he was quiet, maybe said something at the end of the group, but I can't recall what . . .

FRANK   Steve, what mode was this group in?

STEVE   Work, the whole session.

FRANK   I don't see it.

STEVE   You don't? It seems obvious. They dealt with a problem.

FRANK   Last week, you said they were very angry. Today you discover that one member was discharged for doing cocaine. You find out that another member knew but hid it from you. You suspect still another member of having some information that she doesn't want revealed at any cost — you assume she also knew about Ben, but it could just as easily be that she's using coke herself. Virtually no one talked outside of the two people who talk all the time: Howard and Bernice. You can't describe significant participation by anyone else. You're not able to describe what the group was doing while you were talking with Howard and watching Joanne. Yet you tell me it was a working group. My question is: on what?

STEVE   You obviously disagree with my analysis.

FRANK   Sounds to me like a hopeful expectation group, one

that gives the appearance of work, but doesn't accomplish anything.

STEVE   You've lost me.

FRANK   Okay, let's go through it. What was the task of that group?

STEVE   To identify the symptoms of addiction in their experience.

FRANK   And how did the group respond to the task?

STEVE   Well, they didn't . . . because they had to respond to the incident with Ben. And that prevented them from getting to the task, because they were upset.

FRANK   So what did you do to help them get back to the task?

STEVE   I helped them understand that Ben wasn't really in control. . . . I pointed out to them that one of the symptoms of addiction is continued use despite the adverse consequences. That it wasn't really that hard to understand, and it was symptomatic of the disease. That helped them work through their feelings.

FRANK   OK, besides making that one point, what else did you do which brought them closer to the task?

STEVE   Nothing, I guess. I thought the other was more important.

FRANK   What could be more important than the task in a task-oriented group?

STEVE   I just think they were so upset and angry at Ben that they wouldn't have been able to concentrate on anything else.

FRANK   How do you know that? How do you know how they would have responded to an effort to bring them back to task, since you didn't make any?

STEVE   I don't.

FRANK   Instead, you helped draw them off task. You may have thought you were doing the right thing, but it wasn't what you were there to do. Whatever you got accomplished, it wasn't the task.

STEVE   I see.

FRANK   It may be that Joanne was upset because of what

you said. It could also be she's using coke herself. Or that
somebody else is, and they'll get caught. Either way, you
didn't get anywhere near what was going on in that group.

STEVE   Tell me what else I could have done.

FRANK   I think you were so happy they weren't angry with
you that you missed the fact they still weren't working.
They did talk a lot, but not about the task. Some members
showed emotion, but most said little or nothing. You had a
group with *Actives* and *Passives*. It looked like work to
you, but what do you have to show for it? People may feel
better – or more correctly, one or two people feel better –
but what's changed in their understanding of the disease?
As far as I can see, very little.

STEVE   I blew it.

FRANK   You ran into a hopeful expectation group, and they
sold you on the idea that they were doing well when in fact
they weren't. Groups sometimes do that: They aren't
successful, so instead of working harder or dropping out,
they *redefine* success. I remember one group where I
discovered that two members had been drinking for the
entire year they attended the group . . . and most of the
others knew it. The only person they hid it from was the
leader. When I finally confronted them, one of the drinkers
informed me that she had long ago come to accept that her
definition of "sobriety" was different from mine. Hers
included drinking, you see. But she enjoyed the companionship of the group, so she kept coming. It was her compromise: It allowed her to stay in the group while continuing
to drink every so often.

There's no more difficult mode for an inexperienced leader to
spot and to deal with than hopeful expectation. What else
could Steve have tried? Confrontation usually works, as long as
the leader confronts the group rather than the Actives, and
provides them with a clear direction for discussion. In many
instances, a hopeful expectation group will pay lip service to
the idea of working on a task, but in practice will range far and
wide in pursuit of individual attention and tangential issues.

Simply tightening the discussion so that it reflects the stated task often produces the desired result. And as with helpless groups, any attempt to intervene will normally produce a period of hostility (usually active) before a return to work can occur.

Later on the focus turns to Susan, who has led her first solo group.

FRANK   So how did it go?

SUSAN   Strange. I don't know if it was good or bad.

FRANK   What happened?

SUSAN   The group started very slowly . . . there were several minutes of silence. But before I could do much in the way of intervention, Ken and Barry took over. There were some problems – Nancy wanted to talk about how much she disliked her counselor, which was off task – but Ken just told her that wasn't what they were here for, and she let it drop. And then the weirdest thing happened: I found myself just sitting and listening. I kept reminding myself to watch for helplessness or hostility or whatever, but they never showed up for more than brief periods, and the group seemed to get out of it by themselves. I did make a couple of comments, but just to clarify things.

FRANK   Were they on task?

SUSAN   Remarkably so. The most surprising thing was when somebody got off task, the group would bring them back.

FRANK   So what's the problem?

SUSAN   I feel like I didn't *do* anything.

FRANK   You did a lot.

SUSAN   I did?

FRANK   Yes. You let them work. You had an urge to take over, which you resisted. If they'd needed intervention, you could have provided it. But from what I can see, they didn't. They were able to identify and deal with their own problems.

SUSAN   That was a work group, wasn't it?

FRANK   (nods) I think so. And when the group works, your

job is easy. The challenge for the leader is to avoid screwing it up.

SUSAN   Yeah, I really was itching to jump in there and "help." My ACOA personality coming through, I guess.

FRANK   I don't think it has much to do with your upbringing. It springs from the way groups operate. It's like a recipe: Start with a group that doesn't want to work and a leader who wants to "fix" them, and you have all the ingredients for failure. Maybe the most important thing a leader must learn is to recognize her limitations. You can give information, clarify, set boundaries, hold the group on task. But ultimately, success or failure is up to them. Your job is to get them to realize that.

SUSAN   Will they work like that tomorrow?

FRANK   Oh, I doubt it. They'll probably decide they've done enough for one lifetime and need a vacation. But the more time they spend in the work mode, the easier it will be for them to get through helplessness or hostility and back into work. And that's when we begin to speak of them as a working group — one where work has become the preferred mode for the *group* as well as for the leader.

□   □   □

So that's our message. We like to think we have provided an alternative to traditional psychotherapy groups — one which is, we hope, better suited to the realities of recovery from addictive disease. If you adopt some or all of these methods, we believe you will see the appearance of strong groups instead of weak ones. These groups will not be dependent on you or any other designated leader, however. They will truly be "powerful agents for change" in the treatment of a potentially fatal disease.

SUGGESTED READING

ALCOHOLISM

Under the Influence, by James Milam and Katherine Ketcham. Bantam, 1984.
The best explanation of alcoholism as a chronic disease.

The Natural History of Alcoholism, by George Vaillant. Harvard University Press, 1983.
A remarkably intelligent discussion of prospective research on the causes and effects of alcoholism. Lays to rest a considerable number of common misconceptions.

Is Alcoholism Hereditary? by Donald Goodwin. Oxford University Press, 1976.
Goodwin is that rarity: a scientist who can write clearly. Excellent review of available evidence.

COCAINE ADDICTION

800-Cocaine, by Mark Gold. Bantam, 1984.
An excellent overview of the epidemic and the addictive syndrome, aimed at the lay reader.

TREATMENT

Don't Help: A Guide to Working with the Alcoholic, by Ronald Rogers and Chandler Scott McMillin. Madrona Press, 1988.
Describes a method for treating alcoholism and drug dependency as chronic disease rather than character disorder or manifestation of psychosocial problems.

FAMILY

Getting Them Sober, Parts One and Two, by Toby Rice Drews. Bridge Publishing, 1980.
   Good, practical advice for the family member.

Freeing Someone You Love from Alcohol and Other Drugs, by Ronald Rogers and Chandler Scott McMillin. Price, Stern, Sloan, 1989.
   A comprehensive guide to intervention, treatment, and recovery, directed at the family.

INTERVENTION

Living on the Edge, by Katherine Ketcham and Ginny Gustafson. Bantam, 1989.
   A solid introduction to the principles of intervention, aimed at the family member.

Intervention: How to Help Those Who Don't Want Help, by Vernon Johnson. Johnson Institute Press, 1986.
   Includes examples of confrontation sessions.

TWELVE-STEP PROGRAMS

The Twelve Steps Revisited, by Ronald Rogers and Chandler Scott McMillin. Madrona Press, 1988.
   How to use the Twelve Steps from the perspective of treating a chronic disease.

PUBLICATIONS OF ALCOHOLICS ANONYMOUS AND NARCOTICS ANONYMOUS

Alcoholics Anonymous, Bill W. and others, 1955.
   The "bible" of AA. Includes the all-important chapter, "How It Works."

Twelve Steps and Twelve Traditions, Bill W., 1953.
   The "official" interpretation of the Steps and Traditions of AA.

Living Sober, 1975.
   Practical advice for the first days of recovery.

Narcotics Anonymous, 1982.
    NA's version of AA's Big Book.

RECOVERY

Eating Right to Live Sober, L. Ann Mueller and Katherine Ketcham. Bantam, 1986.
    Nutrition and diet for the recovering alcoholic. A useful book for professionals who are encouraging their patients to change eating practices.

Recovering, L. Ann Mueller and Katherine Ketcham. Bantam, 1987.
    Basic review of intervention, treatment, and recovery. Solidly based on a view of alcoholism as a chronic disease.

INDEX

abstinence:
  emphasis on, 69, 150
  prerequisite to participation, 115–17
actively hostile groups, 29–30
active negativism, defense mechanism, 129t
activity, see mode
adaptive tolerance, 7
aftercare group A, 69–76
aftercare group B, 76–85
aggressing, in work groups, 146
Alcoholics Anonymous, 3, 5–6, 58, 112
  as a working group, 6, 147–54
  see also step discussion group; Twelve Traditions
anonymity, 153
authority:
  in Alcoholics Anonymous, 151
  within the group, 14
  in hostile groups, 31–32
  see also leadership; status
autonomy:
  in Alcoholics Anonymous groups, 150–51
  in helpless groups, 25
  in personal decision-making, 84
  in the work mode, 42–43

background climate, 13
  in Alcoholics Anonymous groups, 150
  detox group exercise, 57
  in helpless groups, 25
  in hopeful expectation groups, 35
  hostile, 31
  in working groups, 40–41, 45

bell curves, 121f, 122f, 123f
  self-diagnosis group use of, 120
blocking, in work groups, 146
bonding, 12
  in Alcoholics Anonymous groups, 149–50
  aftercare group A, exercise, 75
  aftercare group B, exercise, 83–84
  defense mechanism group, exercise, 110
  detox group exercise, 56
  first step group, exercise, 93
  in helpless groups, 25
  in hopeful expectation groups, 35
  in hostile groups, 31
  multiple family group, exercise, 103
  around resistance, 16
  step group, exercise, 67
  in the working group, 39
boundaries:
  of treatment groups, 119
  in working groups, 44

chronic disease model, 6–9
  medical rehabilitation, 113
client-centered group therapy, 1–2
climate, 13
  aftercare group A, exercise, 75
  aftercare group B, exercise, 84
  defense mechanism group, exercise, 110
  first step group, exercise, 93
  multiple family group, exercise, 103
  step group, exercise, 67–68
cocaine use, options, 122f
comfort, in helpless groups, 25